THE FIRST AMENDMENT
AND
THE NEWS MEDIA

Final Report

ANNUAL CHIEF JUSTICE EARL WARREN CONFERENCE ON ADVOCACY IN THE UNITED STATES

June 8—9, 1973

Sponsored by

THE ROSCOE POUND-AMERICAN TRIAL LAWYERS FOUNDATION
20 Garden Street, Cambridge, Massachusetts 02138

Library of Congress Catalog Card Number: 73-86879

CONTENTS

3

Foreword

We are a nation in anguish. Events are unfolding before the American people that are causing them to question the integrity of all institutions that comprise this country.

We have a tripartite government that works through a system of checks and balances. And beyond this, the fifty-five men, who framed our Constitution, wisely provided us with a Bill of Rights. Recent history shows us that, through the ingenuity of a free press, ominous government events have been brought to the attention of the public.

But the press itself has become engaged in a conflict with the government over confidentiality. A blizzard of subpoenas were served on novice news people working on local newspapers, as well as experienced journalists, editors and publishers of our country's national press. In the *Branzburg* case the U.S. Supreme Court decreed that newsmen are compelled to reveal confidential sources and to testify before grand juries *(Branzburg v. Hayes*, 408 U.S. 665 (1972)). Following this decision a multitude of bills were introduced in Congress and in various state legislatures to protect newsmen from revealing confidential sources. As of publication of this Conference Report, no federal legislation has passed, even though scores of bills have been introduced. The subject is not an easy one. Journalists differ, legislators argue on either the extent of legal protection or the need for legislation.

When the First Amendment was written into the United States Constitution, it was the first time in history that a nation of people had written into their organic law a provision to assure the press' freedom. The broad language of the First Amendment was believed to make the press absolutely free from restraint before publication. For nearly 200 years, the press functioned in this way. However, in our time we have witnessed prior restraint of publication. (*New York Times Company v. United States*, 403 U.S. 713 (1971)).

This was the position the press found itself in when it was determined that the Annual Chief Justice Earl Warren Conference/1973, sponsored by the Roscoe Pound-American Trial Lawyers Foundation, would be devoted to the discussion of the First Amendment and the news media. Before proceeding with the Conference, we sought the advice of one of America's foremost constitutional scholars, Professor Thomas I. Emerson, Lines Professor of Law at Yale Law School. Professor Emerson is a legal theoretician with an extraordinary understanding and knowledge of the First Amendment. We are deeply grateful to him for his guidance.

The subject — The First Amendment and The News Media — was divided into three parts, each related to the other but each with distinctive problems: (a) Journalist's Privilege; (b) Broadcast Journalism; (c) Access to Government Information.

Careful consideration was given to the selection of the authors of the background papers, which were to be the starting points for discussion. The Foundation is greatly indebted to the three knowledgeable and dedicated professors, who prepared thought-provoking and stimulating papers: Benno C. Schmidt, Jr., Columbia University School of Law on "Journalists' Privilege: One Year After Branzburg"; Sig Mickelson, The Medill School of Journalism, Northwestern University on "The First Amendment and Broadcast Journalism"; and Samuel J. Archibald, Department of Communication, American University on "Access to Government Information — The Right Before The First Amendment." These papers were circulated to all Conferees prior to their gathering at The Roscoe Pound-American Trial Lawyers Research Center in Cambridge on June 8 and June 9. Thus, when they met, they were able to focus immediately on specific points and proceed from there to deeper discussion and conclusions. The background papers did not limit discussion or prejudice thinking. (These background papers follow the Final Recommendations of the Conference in this publication.)

Meeting at the Pound Center for this two-day Conference was a highly diverse, thoughtful and deeply-involved group of people — constitutional law professors, newspaper executives, journalists (including some who had been subpoenaed to testify before grand juries), television broadcasters, television executives, political scientists, lawyers, journalism professors, clergyman, congressional counsels, and judges — our country's first such Conference with so distinguished a group of participants.

In order to give everyone an opportunity to join in free discussion, the Conferees were divided into three groups. Each group discussed the three topics separately, with each of the writers of the background papers present to expand on his written ideas. Following the group meetings, all Conferees met in a plenary session, where the adopted recommendations of each group were discussed and then formulated into a draft of the final Recommendations of the entire Conference.

In a Conference such as this, which brings together articulate people who are forceful in their viewpoints, it is necessary to have discussion leaders who have the ability to lead the group to conclusions. We acknowledge and thank the following people, who served so well as group chairmen: Professor David Haber of Rutgers University School of Law; Professor Barbara D. Underwood of Yale Law School and the Honorable George W. Wood of Charleston, West Virginia.

Our appreciation also goes to those talented people, who were the reporters and who so capably compiled the thinking of the Conference clearly and concisely for written dissemination: Professor Eliot A. Landau of Drake University Law School; Professor Robert M. O'Neil, Vice President and Provost for Academic Affairs, University of Cincinnati and Ronald L. Plesser, Director of the Press Information Center, Washington, D.C.

Following the Conference, a written draft was sent to all Conferees and they were given an opportunity to add their further comments and dissents to be included in the formulation of the Final Report. The majority of the Conferees returned the draft indicating their complete approval; some returned it making merely a note of dissent — without comment — regarding a specific Recommendation; and others noted their dissent along with specific comments. Some dissents, comments and further explanations are set forth in footnotes.

This Final Conference Report is presented in three parts — (a) Journalist's Privilege; (b) Broadcast Journalism; (c) Access to Government Information. A summary prefaces Journalist's Privilege followed by the Recommendations and commentary. Recommendations followed by a commentary are set forth in the other two parts.

A consensus was reached on the three parts of the Conference — Journalist's Privilege, Broadcast Journalism, Access to Government Information. There were two dissenting reports submitted on Broadcast Journalism. Professor Thomas I. Emerson wrote a dissenting report on Recommendations VII, VIII and IX of Broadcast Journalism and Dean Jerome A. Barron dissents on all the Recommendations regarding broadcasting. We chose to publish these dissenting reports in the interest of fairness, future study and research. **The Recommendations are not to be construed as the exact views of all the Conferees; the Conference findings were approved by the majority of the Conferees.**

This Foundation has a deep respect for learning. Its function is to assist in keeping intellectual dialogue alive. When the Recommendations were set forth and submitted to us for publication, we of the Conference Committee were amazed to see such bold, forthright, unprecedented proposals. We were surprised because, when the Conferees first began their discussions, such diverse views surfaced that any form of consensus seemed to be impossible to achieve. The Recommendations are all the more remarkable because here sat the students of American newspaper crises — heirs to a long tradition from Benjamin Harris, whose paper *Publick Occurrences* was suppressed in 1690, to the John Peter Zenger case in 1735, to the present. Some of the Conferees had even personally experienced suppression by the government and were awaiting further court action at the time of the Conference. But, through the two days' exchange of experiences — doubts, hopes and fears — these far-sighted people presented not palliatives to existing problems, but strong innovative Recommendations.

What of Journalists' Privilege? The Recommendations say loud and clear to keep the press free; to protect it with a legal privilege.

What of Broadcast Journalism? The consensus is to free television of government control. Here it is recognized that, while technology has set forth intricate problems, the spirit of a democracy is also strong enough to let this 20th Century marvel operate freely.

And what of Access to Government Information? In recent times only the American people have become aware of classification of documents by our government. They have become sensitive to the impact, scope and meaning of classification of government documents in a democracy. Arbitrary use of classification under the guise of "national security" can subvert democratic institutions. The Recommendations, together with the commentary, indicate a course that will free information which rightfully belongs to the people.

While the Foundation does not take a stand on the issue, it recognizes its responsibility to distribute this publication widely. Journalists may be hesitant and perhaps self-conscious in pursuing discussions or writings on the freedom of the press because the public may think this self-serving. However, we hope that they will assist us in publicizing these Recommendations. This Report is published in the public interest. Every effort must be made to inculcate into our citizens the understanding of the real meaning of freedom of the press and their "right to know." It is only with the public's complete involvement and understanding of a free press that it can be preserved. This freedom so basic to the philosophy of our country cannot be presumed — it must be protected. If there is belief in the strength of our constitutional republic, there should be no fear of freedom of the press. But, if there is fear of what this freedom may reveal, then we are on dangerous ground. Our republic is the oldest in the world. In time of strife reasonable men have not hesitated to assemble to resolve difficulties. It was in this spirit of endeavor that the Foundation chose the subject of The First Amendment and The News Media for this year's Conference.

It is our policy to invite three law students to participate in our conferences. They will be among those called upon in future years to implement what is proposed here. Among the students this year was John Sumberg of Yale Law School, who not only participated in our discussion but worked diligently with us in the preparation of this Conference.

There is one person who is the mainstay of every project and sees that ideas and plans come to fruition. In this regard, we extend our appreciation to Catherine E. Bentis, Executive Director of the Foundation, for her dedication.

To former Chief Justice Earl Warren, we wish him to know the honor it is to have this Conference bear his name each year.

To the men and women who came to Cambridge for this Conference to explore this year's critical subject, we thank you for your sincere efforts to revitalize our constitutional republic.

Herbert H. Bennett
President, The Roscoe Pound-American
Trial Lawyers Foundation

Theodore I. Koskoff
Chairman, Annual Chief Justice
Earl Warren Conference 1973

Stanley E. Preiser
Jack A. Travis
Co-Chairmen

FINAL REPORT

THE FIRST AMENDMENT AND THE NEWS MEDIA

PART A

RECOMMENDATIONS
JOURNALIST'S PRIVILEGE

Summary

(Note: The following condenses the final Recommendations of the Conference on Journalist's Privilege. Specific Recommendations along with commentaries follow this summary.)

The basic proposition, on which the Conferees agreed, was the vital importance of a privilege to protect a journalist's confidential information and sources. It was also agreed that such a privilege should apply with equal force in all types of proceedings — civil and criminal trials, grand jury proceedings, and legislative investigations. While the Conferees believed that both the media and law enforcement agencies could generally be trusted to cooperate with each other, and that journalists would very often volunteer information, a privilege was essential to cover cases in which such cooperation did not or could not exist.

There was much discussion of the form in which the privilege should be embodied. Since the Supreme Court recently held that first amendment constitutional protection was not available, journalists must now turn to the legislatures. The Conferees unanimously favored a comprehensive federal shield law, which would supersede less protective state laws but would not prevent states from being more protective if they chose. On the other hand, the majority of the Conferees felt that a diluted or qualified federal law would probably be worse than no law at all.

Who is a journalist? This question is obviously important in defining the scope of the privilege and received some attention from the Conference. The participants rejected on one hand a narrow technical definition, and refused on the other hand to make the privilege available to any person calling himself a journalist. Instead, they agreed that a journalist for purposes of the privilege should be defined as any person regularly employed in a newsgathering capacity by any newspaper or other periodic medium, or any person who has previously published in such a medium, or who is a scholar or researcher in a bona fide capacity with the intent to disseminate.

The final issue, on which considerable time was spent, was whether the privilege should be qualified or absolute. Here the Conference was evenly divided. However, the Conferees rejected all of the proposed exceptions to the privilege — for observed crimes, for information about future crimes (even involving the possible loss of life), for libel suits, and for information sought or needed by the defense in a criminal trial. Although the privilege was left in fact unqualified at the end of the session, the Conference stopped just short of endorsing in principle an absolute journalist's privilege.

I

A journalist should be accorded a legally-protected privilege to include confidential information and sources against compelled testimony.

(Adopted overwhelmingly)

Commentary: The Conferees agreed on a basic journalist's privilege as a guarantor of a free and effective press. The primary interest to be served is not the personal privacy or professional advantage of the reporter, but the flow of information from sensitive sources to the reading public. There was substantial agreement that (as recent empirical studies have shown) much information simply would not be shared with the media, and thus would never reach the public, if disclosure could be indiscriminately compelled. The Conferees cautioned that the *absence* of a privilege would seldom serve the interests of law enforcement, since the drying up of sensitive sources would simply keep the information out of everyone's hands. Thus, one Conferee, remarked, "the *prosecution* won't get the complete information either way. The only question is whether the *public* will have at least partial access."

Recognition of the privilege carried an important corollary: the group generally felt that the press has a sense of responsibility and would avoid most collisions and abuses of any privilege. Many in the group felt that reporters do work closely with the police and prosecution — on whom they in turn depend for certain kinds of information — and do volunteer much information that does not openly breach confidences. Thus, assertion of the privilege should imply no conflict between media and law enforcement officials, but simply a last-resort protection for the rare case in which cooperation breaks down.

During the general discussion, time was also devoted to the status of the press as an industry under governmental regulation. There was implicit recognition that certain aspects of newsgathering and dissemination, though constitutionally protected, were nonetheless subject to governmental regulation. The application to the media of the antitrust laws, repeatedly upheld by the Supreme Court, afford one example. Also, cases holding the press subject to child labor, minimum wage and other general welfare laws are pertinent.

II

For the purpose of the privilege, a journalist should be defined as any person regularly employed in a news-gathering capacity by any newspaper or other periodic publication or broadcast medium, or any person who has previously published in any such medium, or who is a scholar or researcher in a bona fide capacity with the intent to disseminate.[1]

(Adopted by substantial majority)

Commentary: Whether qualified or unqualified, the identification of persons eligible to claim the privilege is essential. At first the definition proposed for consideration was: "Any person regularly employed in a news-gathering capacity by any newspaper or other periodic publication or broadcast medium, or who has a record of prior publication in any such medium." This definition seemed a bit too narrow. Consideration was given to a catch-all addendum such as "and such other persons as the court finds are working in journalistic employment," but that combination was defeated by a substantial margin. The alternative, adopted by a substantial majority, was to add the following language, "and scholars and researchers in a bona fide capacity with the intent to disseminate." By this addendum the Conferees clearly evinced their desire to carry the privilege beyond printed periodicals and the broadcast media to include scholars, pamphleteers, underground publications, and other less traditionally-protected channels of communication and expression.

The Conferees did reject a wholly subjective test when asked to consider whether the privilege should apply to "anyone who says he is a journalist and is engaged in journalistic activity," thus leaving the definition entirely to the claimant. This approach was decisively rejected, thereby underscoring the Conferees' preference for a middle ground between the wholly objective and the completely subjective determination of eligibility.

---

1. Two Conferees, Mr. William G. Mullen and Mr. David Lightman, expressed strong feelings that the definition of a journalist should be extended further. Mr. Lightman was of the opinion that a freelance journalist or a journalist who is publishing for the first time should be included. Mr. Mullen believed that publishers and editors, not specifically working in a "news-gathering capacity," as well as freelance journalists and freelance photographers, should be included.

III

The Journalist's Privilege should be unqualified, that is, the decision whether and to what extent a journalist will testify regarding his sources or the confidential information in his possession should be entirely his own decision.[1]

(Members of the Conference were evenly divided on this Recommendation.)

Commentary: The discussion of this Recommendation required some understanding of the terms "qualified" and "unqualified." The privilege would be *unqualified,* for example, if a journalist could simply refuse to appear before a tribunal, or could appear but refuse to answer any questions, or could make his own determination whether a particular matter was privileged. If, however, the journalist could be compelled to divulge some kinds of information — for example, information gained by personal observation of a crime or knowledge about the sources of libelous statements — then the privilege was clearly *qualified.* Because of the even division on this question, no clear Conference position emerged. Sentiment favoring a completely unqualified privilege was substantial.

The tie vote on this issue created a quandary. Discussion of details and exceptions appeared premature since no clear majority had advocated *any* qualifications. Yet, everyone seemed to agree that details should be discussed, if only for practical reasons. As the Report shows in succeeding pages, the Conferees voted on specific EXCEPTIONS but each one was defeated.

---

1. Mr. Warren Weaver dissented and expressed the opinion that advocating an absolute privilege would be unrealistic and unworkable.

IV

The Journalist's Privilege should extend to all unpublished materials (notes, out-takes, etc.), whether or not containing information acquired in confidence.

(Adopted overwhelmingly)

Commentary: There was concern about demands for several different forms of newsgathering products — written materials, sound recordings, photographs or negatives, and out-takes of television news reports or documentaries. Particular emphasis was placed on the "Selling of the Pentagon" experience, as an indication of the hazards of compelled disclosure in this area. Also recognized was the protection of journalistic and scholarly creativity by safeguarding the process at its most vulnerable point, *i.e.* prepublication working material.

V

The Journalist's Privilege, as outlined in Recommendations I, II and IV, should be embodied in a new Federal law to include the following:

A. It would supplement, but would not imply the absence of, First Amendment protection for the privilege;

B. It would preempt less protective but not more protective State laws;

C. It would not preclude additional protection through the courts.

If Congress did not enact the body of law advocated above, then no new Federal legislation should be adopted with regard to the privilege.

(Adopted overwhelmingly)

Commentary: The Conferees recommended congressional adoption of a broad shield law. There was substantial fear that the adoption of a limited shield law would be counterproductive, leaving the journalist less protected than he would be when relying on the Court's future interpretation of the First Amendment. The Conference overwhelmingly agreed that the journalist should be protected, but there was some reluctance to turn to legislatures for that protection. Many Conferees felt that the legislative process might produce a far too limited protection. If Congress does not pass a broad shield law, it was the conclusion of the Conference that no shield law should be adopted.

Among the arguments in favor of a broad federal shield law was the "invitation" to formulate legislation which the Supreme Court seemed to give in *Branzburg v. Hayes,* 408 U.S. 665 (1972). In the view of the majority of the Court, creation of and definition of evidentiary privileges seemed a proper function of legislatures rather than of judges. In other contexts, too, courts have been reluctant to recognize any new privileges or to extend those already on the books without explicit authority from the legislature.

Several considerations may, however, argue against legislation. A few journalists at the Conference feared that efforts to obtain new protective laws might appear to be "special pleading" and would thus jeopardize public support of the media and the press. Others feared that enactment of legislation covering some journalistic activities might imply the exclusion of others and thus dilute the force and scope of first amendment protection. To base such legislation on the Commerce Clause (as might seem necessary in light of *Branzburg*) may present the media as being involved more in commercial than intellectual and creative activities.[1] Also, if a shield law were once enacted and later repealed, the journalist's position might well be worse than if no legislation were ever adopted in the first place. Finally, a number of Conferees seemed to feel that the field was so complex, and so beset with distinctions, qualifications and exceptions, that it was wiser to stay out of the legislative thicket altogether.

In view of these arguments, the Conference approached proposals for legislation quite cautiously. It was understood that any federal law would have to preempt the state laws that were *less protective*, but would not preclude states from adopting *broader privileges*. Congressional action now would also be without prejudice to any subsequent and favorable protection by the courts, either on constitutional or nonconstitutional grounds. Moreover, any legislation should proceed on the assumption that *Branzburg* may well be modified or even overruled, and thus should not imply the absence of eventual first amendment protection for the journalist's sources.

VI

Regardless of statutory or judicial safeguards, all law enforcement officers and grand juries should exercise a high degree of self-restraint, seeking information from journalists only when necessary to serve strong governmental interests and only when the information is unavailable elsewhere.

(Adopted overwhelmingly)

Commentary: The discussion of form or method of protection included one other element. Early in the plenary session there was reference to the value of self-restraint in information-gathering. The Conferees overwhelmingly supported the view that law enforcement officials should subpoena information from journalists only in very special cases, where the information was vital to an important governmental interest and could be obtained in no other way. Yet, most of the participants recognized that since self-restraint could not always be expected, more practical and immediate protection would be necessary for the working journalist.

---

1. Professor Albert J. Rosenthal states: "The legislation would not have to be based on the Commerce Clause. Congress can control procedures in federal courts and administrative bodies and before its own committees, and can extend first amendment protections in state proceedings beyond court formulations, pursuant to its power to implement the Fourteenth Amendment, under *Katzenbach v. Morgan.*"

SCOPE OF THE JOURNALIST'S PRIVILEGE

(The Conferees considered and DEFEATED the following specific Recommendations, which were proposed as EXCEPTIONS to the Journalist's Privilege.)

A

An exception to the Journalist's Privilege should be created where a journalist has been an eyewitness to a crime of violence.

(Defeated overwhelmingly)

Commentary: The case contemplated by this exception would be the following: A reporter gains admission to a building or office to cover one event or story under a pledge of confidence and, while there, observes a crime of violence unrelated to the events or activities that justified the entry. Even though compelled disclosure might not directly breach the confidential relationship, the Conferees felt the policies of the privilege sufficiently strong that no such exception should be allowed.[1]

---

1. Mr. Weaver expressed his dissent. He commented: "I do not support this any more than I believe that the general principle of confidentiality of presidential records should permit Richard Nixon to deny evidence on criminal activity to the Watergate grand jury."

B

An exception to the Privilege should be created where a journalist has observed a crime involving loss of life.

(Defeated overwhelmingly)

Commentary: Since this exception would be somewhat narrower than the rejected exception for any crime of violence, the case for relaxing the privilege might seem stronger. Most of the Conferees felt, however, that even where observed loss of life was involved, the case for compelled disclosure was clearly outweighed by the need for confidentiality.

C

An exception to the Privilege should be created where a journalist has received information about a threat of future harm to the life of another person.

(Defeated narrowly)

Commentary: By far the closest vote came on this Recommendation of whether the Privilege applied to a journalist possessing any information concerning a threat to someone's life. Under circumstances where even the attorney-client privilege might yield, a bare majority of the Conferees was unwilling to override a journalist's privilege. While there was consensus that a responsible reporter would typically volunteer information of this sort or warn the victim, the Privilege should still apply if the journalist wished to claim it in order to protect a source.[1]

---

1. Mr. Weaver expressed the following opinion: "The idea that a citizen's responsibility to observe and enforce the criminal laws, thereby promoting the public safety, can somehow be obscured or even vitiated by his claimed status as a recorder of history — talk about irony! — is patent nonsense, and its assertion weakens the cause of promoting the maximum reasonable freedom for such observers."

D

An exception to the Privilege should be created for all civil and criminal trials.

(Defeated overwhelmingly)

Commentary: While most of the discussion and litigation over the Privilege relates to grand jury investigations, similar issues may arise in other forums. Information may be demanded in the course of pre-trial discovery (as in the Judy Garland case of some years ago, *Garland v. Torre*, 259 F.2d 545 (2d Cir.), *cert. denied*, 358 U.S. 910 (1958)), or during legislative hearings — as with the "Selling of the Pentagon" controversy — or in later stages of a criminal prosecution.

In the *Garland* case, a plaintiff in a civil libel suit tried to use discovery proceedings to determine the source of a statement in a newspaper column attributed to an unnamed network executive. When the reporter refused to identify her source, the federal court sentenced her to jail for contempt. In the Pentagon episode, a congressional committee tried to obtain out-takes of a network television program dealing with publicity and promotional activities of the Defense Department. When network executives refused to surrender the unused footage to the committee, a contempt citation was considered but never actually voted by Congress.

The question of *whether the privilege should not apply in all trials* brought forth one of the most decisive votes of the Conference. By an overwhelming margin, the Conferees rejected *this proposed limitation.*

E

An exception to the Privilege should be created where a demand is made for information relevant to the defense in a criminal proceeding.

(Defeated by substantial margin)

Commentary: Even though the preparation or presentation of a criminal defense might be made more difficult by the withholding of the requested information, a balancing of the interests seemed clearly to favor the maintenance of the Privilege.

F

An exception to the Privilege should be created where a demand is made for information necessary to the defense in a criminal proceeding, and where said information is available from no other source.

(Defeated narrowly)

Commentary: The Conferees recognized that this proposed exception raised a direct conflict between two sets of constitutional interests — the freedom of the press on the one hand, and the criminal defendant's Sixth Amendment interest in a fair trial on the other hand. Nonetheless, a close majority of the Conferees concluded the Privilege should not yield. In reaching this conclusion, the Conference realized that dismissal of the indictment might often follow the failure of the defendant to obtain such information from a journalist. There was, however, no explicit discussion of that consequence, nor was that result inevitable in the minds of the participants.

G

An exception to the Privilege should be created for all libel actions.

(Defeated overwhelmingly)

Commentary: After rejecting this proposed exception for all libel actions as being far too broad, the Conference then considered a much narrower question: "In a libel suit, should the claiming of the privilege result in an instruction to the jury that it may consider the refusal to testify in deciding whether the plaintiff has met the burden of proof with regard to such issues as truth versus falsehood or (if applicable) proof of actual malice?"

During the discussion, it was suggested that, when a journalist claimed a privilege in a libel suit, that might be a proper subject for adverse comment by the opposing lawyer. (The Supreme Court held several years ago that, in a criminal trial, the prosecution cannot comment unfavorably on the defendant's refusal to testify. Such a comment would undermine the privilege against self-incrimination.) It was assumed that the defendant in the suit was the person who had made or written the defamatory statement. If the defendant were some other person — for example, a publisher or distributor of the defamatory words of an author not involved in the case — the situation would be different. The possibility of adverse comment or an unfavorable instruction would make sense only if the defendant were, in fact, the maker of the statement which gave rise to the suit.

PART B

RECOMMENDATIONS
BROADCAST JOURNALISM

(Note: The Recommendations emanating from the discussion on Broadcast Journalism form an integrated whole. Therefore, all the Recommendations appear first and the commentary encompassing these follow. Reference sources are indicated by Note numbers and appear following the commentary.)

VII

In view of the wide spectrum of radio frequencies now available throughout the nation for the expression of a divergency of views, the Federal Communications Act should be amended to remove from the Federal Communications Commission the power to regulate the program content of radio stations.[1]

(Adopted by overwhelming majority)

---

1. Professor Thomas I. Emerson voiced an opposing opinion to Recommendations VII, VIII and IX. See statement on page 30. Professor Barbara D. Underwood holds similar views. Dean Jerome A. Barron, who disagrees with the Recommendations on Broadcast Journalism, sets forth his opinion on page 31. Professor David Haber dissents from Recommendations VII, VIII and IX, and concurs with the statements of Professor Emerson and Dean Barron.

VIII

In order to foster freedom of expression, as it exists outside the electronic media, the Federal Communications Act should be amended so as to remove from the Federal Communications Commission all power to regulate the program content of television.[1]

(Adopted by majority)

IX

The Federal Communications Commission should suspend, on an experimental basis, program content regulation of television in limited geographical market areas if total deregulation of television program content cannot be had.

(Adopted by overwhelming majority)

---

1. Mr. Weaver disagreed with the Conference, explaining "that the radio and television situations are distinguishable, that the relatively small number of TV outlets, coupled with their immense audience (compared to newpapers) warrants a much more cautious approach to complete freedom from federal regulation of program content."

X

In order to maximize the diversity of free expression, government should use its anti-monopoly powers to oppose the concentration of media ownership within all identifiable geographical market areas. This includes taking steps not only to prevent concentration, but to more affirmatively reduce existing concentration of ownership.

(Adopted by overwhelming majority)

Commentary on Broadcast Journalism

Commentary: The Conferees placed particular emphasis on the evolved form and substance of the "Fairness Doctrine" (Note 1) as a serious infringement on freedom of expression under the First Amendment. The Doctrine has a two-pronged purpose: It requires stations to cover issues of controversy and public importance and it requires them to present different viewpoints on such issues. A consensus emerged as to the ultimate ideal goal: *freedom for each and every form and portion of the media to choose the mode and content of its own expression.* While much of the group discussion time was devoted to problems involving the Fairness Doctrine and the related problems of "equal time" and "public access," when it came to decide on Recommendations, there was a clear rejection of any regulatory schema based on the Doctrine and of any modification of it other than complete abrogation. The Conferees chose to endorse experimental deregulation rather than to suggest any particular modification of the present regulatory structure.

Conferees stressed a strong resistance to the ever-growing extent of regulation, from significant recent advances in technology, and from omnipresent concern over the potential of government to twist the electronic media's collective arm.

In its infancy, governmental regulation of the broadcast media was limited to technical matters, mostly revolving around allocating frequencies. There were more than enough frequencies available. The government's role then was mostly that of a traffic officer, permitting each station to go in its own direction, so long as it did not collide with another. Ironically, it was the very increase in the number and diversity of radio stations in the 1920's, which brought about the greater regulation which is now seen as a threat to the media's freedom of expression. The Federal Communications Commission (FCC) completed the conversion of broadcast regulation from mere traffic control of privately-owned stations into a system for controlling content in *Mayflower Broadcasting Corp.* when it relied on the limited number of frequencies to restrain editorializing by the station's owner.[1] Under this system, a licensee is obligated to devote a reasonable percentage of broadcast time to issues of public importance, to present different and opposing positions on such issues, to seek out spokespersons for views opposing its own, and (upon request) to make time available for the presentation of those opposing views (Note 2). By applying these tests broadly, both in individual cases and more generally in license renewal proceedings, the Commission has succeeded in confirming the tendency of the courts to exalt the FCC euphemism that its decisions "foster self-regulation." The result is that the courts and the FCC rely on the euphemism rather than to seriously face up to the governmental censorship which has resulted.

---

1. Professor Eliot A. Landau adds the following historical perspective: "The Radio Act of 1927 responded to the increased competition for available frequencies by transmuting government's role as a traffic controller to that of a 'protector' whose benefits were to be bestowed only on those applicants who would be responsive to the public 'convenience, interest or necessity'. Even though attempts in Congress to also attach a 'fairness' standard failed, the Federal Radio Commission soon forged one of its own which the courts approved. See, especially, *Great Lakes Broadcasting Co.*, 3 F.R.C. Ann. Rep. 32-33 (1929), *rev'd on other grounds*, 37 F.2d 993 (D.C. Cir. 1930), *cert. dismissed,* 281 U.S. 706; and *KFKB Broadcasting Co. v. Fed. Radio Comm.*, 47 F.2d 670 (D.C. Cir. 1931). The basic provisions of the 1927 Act were incorporated into the present law, again without a 'fairness' standard. Once again, the regulatory body (the newly formed FCC), read the 'public convenience, interest and necessity' clause of the 1934 Act so as to require 'fairness'. See 47 U.S.C. § § 303, 307(a) and 309(a), as applied in *Young People's Assn. for the Propagation of the Gospel*, 6 FCC 178 (1938)."

Most of the Conferees discussed the Fairness Doctrine and came to inconclusive results. Many took a view similar to Winston Churchill's on democracy, *i.e.*, that it was the worst form of government, but the best now available. Some saw it as a temporary measure until better concepts of public access could be developed. Still others saw general value in it, especially when applied to extreme cases of abuse by licensees (Note 3). But one approach did surface in each of the group discussions which ultimately became the basis of the Recommendations.

Two underlying questions were repeatedly posed. *Whose* right of free expression is to be protected? Why must *each* station satisfy public fairness or access needs?

The Supreme Court had already given its answers:

> ... *It is the right of the viewers and listeners, not the right of the broadcasters, which is paramount* ... It is the purpose of the First Amendment to preserve an uninhibited market place of ideas in which truth will ultimately prevail, rather than to countenance monopolization of that market, whether it be by the Government itself or a private licensee ... It is the right of the public to receive suitable access to social, political, esthetic, moral, and other ideas and experiences which is crucial here. (Note 4) (Emphasis added.)
>
> It does not violate the First Amendment to treat licensees given the privilege of using scarce radio frequencies as proxies for the entire community, obligated to give suitable time and attention to matters of great public concern. To condition the granting or renewal of licenses on a willingness to present representative community views on controversial issues is consistent with the ends and purposes of those constitutional provisions forbidding the abridgement of freedom of speech and freedom of the press. Congress need not stand idly by and permit those with licenses to ignore the problems which beset the people or to exclude from airways anything but their own views of fundamental questions. The statute, long administrative practice, and cases are to this effect. (Note 5)

But must we settle for the common blandness and lack of diversity in programming which has been the result of these benighted efforts? The answer was found in challenging the entire regulatory structure.

The necessary assumption is the uniqueness of the electronic media as "modes of expression" due to the limited nature of access by virtue of having only a finite number of frequencies to allocate (Note 6). But this "uniqueness" is no longer true, if indeed it ever were so. As of 1971, there were about 7,284 radio stations in the

United States and about 1,013 television stations, for a total of 8,297 broadcast outlets. By way of contrast, there were only 1,749 daily newspapers in 1971.[1]

Another comparison is media availability in relevant geographic market areas. In every state, the availability of broadcast media is signficantly greater than that of daily newspapers.

Scarcity of electronic media frequencies and facilities is an old adage. And the newer technological developments in cable antenna television (CATV) have further eroded the scarcity argument.

Many of the Conferees expect that CATV, in the not too distant future, will provide most viewers with an extremely large choice of programming.[2] In addition, the FCC regulations for CATV licensing provide greater opportunities for public access to television through the requirement of reserving channels for locally-originated programming and use.

Therefore, the "scarcity" or "uniqueness" theory can no longer rationally be invoked to support special regulation of the broadcast media different from that of the press.[3] This is the critical conclusion from which the Conference Recommendations flow. If deprived of this rationale, the "public utility" approach cannot stand.

When deprived of the "public utility" approach, Congress and the courts must return to the First Amendment and apply it for the benefit of *all the media*. Traditional first amendment theory would clearly prohibit any governmental action burdening a licensee's right of free expression (Note 7). The right of free expression is that of the station owners, who are licensed to use the airwaves as newspaper publishers receive special permits for reduced rate use of the mails.

---

1. Professor Landau believes a point should be made here to answer the concern over access and would add: "In a purely pragmatic sense, it is at least as difficult today to create a major new newspaper or magazine as it is to set up a television station, and much more difficult than a radio station."

2. Mr. Tracy Westen pointed out, "CATV will not necessarily provide a greater choice of programming. At most, CATV systems will bring in existing television signals from other markets—and these are often the same network or syndicated programs that are being broadcast in the CATV's own market."

3. Mr. Lawrence M. Baskir wished this Report to give the "rarely expressed argument in favor of regulation." He explained: "It is not scarcity but power which moves so many — whether liberal or conservative — to favor regulation. Both in Congress and elsewhere, the extraordinary impact TV has on viewers in shaping attitudes produces great opposition to the idea that this instrument should be left in the uncontrolled hands of private interests, especially since those interests are already economically so massive."

At the same time diversity of expression is not to be found in a tightly-regulated medium, where fears of censorship, governmental interference, and the possibility of losing one's license reduce creativity to a common blandness, so as not to incur the wrath of the regulator.[1] Diversity shall come from the presence of a multiplicity of broadcasting voices, each competing for an audience in the open marketplace of ideas. No efforts to please a sponsor, who may have low standards, can ever match the coercive effect of stifling regulation. (There was recognition of non-commercial television's attempt to provide quality and diversity.)

To better assure the desired diversity, the Conferees urged strong enforcement of the anti-trust laws. The more people involved in medium ownership, the greater will be the number of voices and the greater the chance of having significantly different voices.

Conferees did not believe there should be concentrated ownership of multiple outlets in particular relevant geographic market areas.[2] However, it was concluded that no new laws or changes in laws are needed. The existing anti-trust laws and other legal authorities for regulation of competition are strong enough and the courts have shown themselves willing and desirous of having the FCC implement them.[3]

---

1. Professor L. A. (Scot) Powe, Jr. states: "There are at least two instances of creative programming being aired and getting the licensee in trouble with the FCC. I would suggest *Jack Straw Foundation* 21 FCC 2d 833 (1970) (one year renewal) *reconsidered,* 29 FCC 2d 334 (1971) (three year renewal). Although *Jack Straw* was sanctioned, the hearing examiner found its programming 'outstanding'. The other cite I would recommend is *Eastern Education Radio*, 24 FCC 408 (1970)."

2. Professor Nathanial L. Nathanson commented: "The FCC has ample authority to eliminate such concentration of ownership if it wishes to do so."

3. Regarding the FCC's role, Mr. Westen added: "The existing 'anti-trust laws' may be strong enough in theory, but the FCC has generally refused to enforce them. The FCC has expressly stated that it cannot 'enforce' the anti-trust laws — that it is the function of the Justice Department to do so. Moreover, the FCC has consistently adopted measures that would *decrease* media diversity — such as its 'Policy Statement on Comparative Renewals', which was overturned by the courts in 1971."

Professor Powe concurs: "The existing anti-trust laws are strong enough if the FCC will show itself willing to implement them in cases involving renewal applications, transfer requests, as well as initial applications for licenses."

In sum then, a clear majority of the Conferees believe that the fact of great electronic media diversity and participation, which exists today, has destroyed the use of any "scarcity" concept as a justification for regulation based on a "public utility" theory. It is only the comparatively lesser diversity of television as compared with radio and some uncertainties over what may yet come from CATV, which has led a sizeable minority of the Conferees to resist deregulation of the program content of television and urge the adoption of an experimental program. The absence of any such limiting factors as to radio explains the overwhelming vote for immediately deregulating the program content of radio stations. Deconcentrating media ownership stems from the Conferees' general desire to assure greater diversity in media expression,[1] as well as the feeling of some that this would be even more crucial if the other Recommendations were implemented.

Under the Conference proposals, the role of the FCC would be restored to what the majority of Conferees felt it should be: a traffic controller for the airwaves.

---

1. The Conference did not explore either in the group discussions or at the plenary session the news media as related to minority groups. Mr. Westen wanted this Final Report to reflect this fact and stated that "consumer and minority groups have been fighting for years to make television more responsive to community needs — including hiring of minorities, program service in Spanish, and program service to the poor and other minorities, who cannot afford to buy sponsors' products and who are, therefore, excluded from programming."

Mr. Baskir would also like to have seen discussion regarding "complaints of minority groups that they are denied access to broadcasting." He pointed out: "They complain of the refusal of stations to cover their views or to sell time to them. Some have also argued for a first amendment right to equal access independent of ability to pay for time.

"Proponents of this view, advocated strongly by Professor Jerome Barron and the United Church of Christ (Rev. Dr. Everett Parker) seek to establish an affirmative obligation, enforced by the federal government, to allocate access to 'nonestablishment' opinion. They seek more, rather than less, regulation to effectuate the purposes of the First Amendment."

Mr. Baskir believes that deregulation will provide no assurance that minority opinions can have access to the media.

Notes to Commentary on Broadcast Journalism

1. While the genesis of the Doctrine can be traced back to the Radio Act of 1927, its effective start is found in *Report of the Commission in the Matter of Editorializing by Broadcast Licensees*, 13 FCC 1246 (1949). It was codified in the 1959 Act, which amended 47 U.S.C. § 315, and was upheld against constitutional challenge in *Red Lion Broadcasting Corp. v. FCC*, 395 U.S. 367, 383-87 (1969). See also *Columbia Broadcasting System, Inc. v. Democratic National Committee*, 412 U.S.   , 93 S.Ct. 2080, 36 L.Ed. 2d 772 (1973).

2. Ibid. at 1249-51. See also *Green v. FCC*, 447 F.2d 323 (D.C. Cir. 1970); *Metropolitan Broadcasting Corp.*, 40 FCC 491 (1959); *Obligation of Broadcast Licensees under the Fairness Doctrine*, 23 FCC 2d 27 (1970); and *In Re Applicability of the Fairness Doctrine in the Handling of Controversial Issues of Public Importance, Public Notice — B*, 29 Fed. Reg. 10415 (July 25, 1964).

3. Most often cited were the Lamar Broadcasting case (*Office of Communication of the United Church of Christ v. FCC*, 425 F.2d 543, 138 U.S. App. D.C. 112 (1969)); and the Rev. Carl McIntyre case (*Brandywine-Maine Line Radio, Inc. v. FCC*, 473 F.2d 16 (D.C. Cir. 1973)).

4. *Red Lion Broadcasting Corp. v. FCC*, 395 U.S. 367, 390 (1969).

5. *Ibid.* at 394.

6. *National Broadcasting Co. v. United States*, 319 U.S. 190, 226 (1943), held:

> Unlike other modes of expression, radio inherently is not available to all. That is its unique characteristic, and that is why, unlike other modes of expression, it is subject to governmental regulation.

7. See, *e.g.*, *Near v. Minnesota*, 283 U.S. 697 (1931); *Mills v. Alabama*, 384 U.S. 214 (1966); and *New York Times Co. v. United States* (the Pentagon Papers case), 403 U.S. 713 (1971). But see, *Red Lion, loc. cit.*

Dissent From Specific Recommendations on Broadcast Journalism
Professor Thomas I. Emerson

I strongly dissent from Recommendations VII, VIII and IX to "deregulate" the radio and television media. The stated purpose is to create "freedom for each and every form and portion of the media to choose the mode and content *of its own expression.*" In my judgment this approach embodies a very limited view of the real impact of total decontrol upon the system of free expression in this country. There is no assurance whatever that abandonment of the Fairness Doctrine, of the rules for encouraging diversification in programming, or of similar FCC requirements would result in greater diversity of expression or increased access for persons wishing to use the broadcast media. On the contrary, the result would only be to assure a continuing monopoly of expression to existing owners and operators of the broadcasting facilities.

The underlying factual premise for decontrol — that a scarcity of broadcasting facilities no longer exists — seems to me unfounded. The Supreme Court's analysis in the *Red Lion* case on this issue is far more convincing than the statement of the majority. For example, the excess of radio and television stations over newspapers signifies very little. A better comparison would be that between the number of radio and television stations and the number of printing presses. The truth is that, even aside from economic factors, the physical characteristics of the electronic media, at least under the present scheme of regulation, limit access to those relatively few who are licensed to operate a station or who are given permission by a licensee.

Moreover, the majority's constitutional premises seem to me similarly defective. The Supreme Court's decision in *Red Lion*, affirmed in *Columbia Broadcasting*, makes it plain that the main thrust of the First Amendment in this area is to protect the rights of "the viewers and listeners" and the "entire community," not "to countenance the monopolization" of the marketplace of ideas.

Nor does it appear at all likely that the anti-trust laws, which have prevented increasing concentration in the press, can ever be successfully invoked to assure free and open use of the broadcast media.

There is, of course, a continuing problem of the inhibiting effect of government controls upon the broadcast media. No one can ignore this. But the broadcast industry, by taking a staunch position in defense of its rights, carries within itself the power to counteract many of these effects of the control system. The more important problem, at this time, from the overall viewpoint of maintaining a healthy system of free expression, is the lack of access to the broadcast media by persons and groups with differing points of view. The Fairness Doctrine and similar requirements are not an entirely satisfactory answer to this problem. Until some better devices are adopted, however, abandonment of such controls would narrow rather than expand freedom of expression in broadcasting.

Dissent From Recommendations on Broadcast Journalism
Dean Jerome A. Barron

The gist of the Recommendations on Broadcast Journalism appears to be that scarcity of outlets is less of a problem in the electronic media than in the print media and that, since the print media are not regulated, the electronic media should not be regulated either. With regard to this latter point, it should be pointed out that the question of whether the print media have any obligations to provide a right of reply is hardly a settled issue. The Supreme Court of Florida has just recently sustained as entirely consistent with the First Amendment the Florida right of reply statute, *Tornillo v. The Miami Herald Publishing Co.*, Supreme Court of Florida, Case No. 43,009, dated July 18, 1973.[1]

In *Rosenbloom v. Metromedia*, 403 U.S. 29 (1971), in the plurality opinion for the Court written by Mr. Justice Brennan and joined in by Mr. Justice Blackmun and Chief Justice Burger, right of reply legislation was both advocated and endorsed as consistent with the First Amendment.

The recent Supreme Court decision in *Columbia Broadcasting System, Inc. v. Democratic National Committee*, 93 S. Ct. 2080 (1973) was a resounding endorsement of the Fairness Doctrine. The Recommendations of the Conference are premised on an identity between first amendment rights and property concepts. Thus, the Conference Recommendations on Broadcast Journalism state on this point as follows:

> The right of free expression is that of the station owners, who are licensed to use
> the airwaves as newspaper publishers receive special permits for reduced rate use
> of the mails. (See page 26.)

In my view, this is not the real nature of the licensee's interest in first amendment protection. The exclusive purpose of the First Amendment is not to isolate from social and legal responsibility those who are in the communications industry.

No one has suggested deregulation to the point of revoking the licenses of all the existing licensees and starting again. On the contrary, the implicit assumption of all pleas for deregulation is that those who are already licensed shall continue on indefinitely with their governmentally-bestowed franchises. In other words, the use of government to shield the present owners and managers of the broadcast media from new entrants is perfectly acceptable. What is apparently unacceptable is compliance with any structure designed to assure an opportunity to be heard to those vast and disparate sectors of the population who do not own or manage media properties.

---

1. This case was decided in July, 1973, following the Conference. The *Miami Herald* appealed and, at press time, the case is on a petition for rehearing before the Supreme Court of Florida.

It is true that the final Recommendation on Broadcast Journalism of the Conference calls upon anti-trust policy to provide diversity of opinion in the broadcast industry. But anti-trust policy in the past has failed to produce that diversity of ideas in broadcasting which it is now called upon to produce. Furthermore, no inconsistency is seen in calling upon government to provide a structure for ownership and competition in broadcasting, when at the same time all kinds of objections are raised when government regulation calls for a structure for debate in broadcasting.

The fundamental assumption is that diversity of opinion must inevitably result if the number of broadcast outlets is increased or if anti-trust policy is vigorous. Both of these developments, of course, would be welcomed. But on that general assumption, the following remarks are, I think, apposite:

> *The merit of programming standards should not depend upon whether radio is no longer a limited access medium or whether television still is. Diversity of ideas, not multiplicity of forums, is the primary objective of the First Amendment.* To be sure, it is hoped that a greater number of forums will create a more diverse opinion process. A flick of the radio dial should be sufficient to dispel that illusion, however. An abundance of radio stations no more guarantees diversity of opinion than scarcity of television stations assures one-sidedness. (Emphasis supplied).   Barron, *An Emerging Right of Access to the Media?* 37 Geo. Wash. L. Rev. 487 at 498 (1969)

The First Amendment does have an affirmative dimension. The meaning of the First Amendment is not exhausted in the imposition of *negative* limitations on government. Professor Emerson has described the first amendment affirmative approach as it relates to broadcasting as follows:

> Quite apart from the scarcity factor in radio and television facilities, it is possible to fashion a theory of control out of affirmative concepts of the First Amendment. The regulations we are here concerned with are not those designed to restrict expression on behalf of other social interests. They are intended to promote the system of free expression through encouraging wider participation by those who wish to communicate and greater diversity for those who wish to hear. In general, the affirmative features of the First Amendment would permit this.   Emerson, THE SYSTEM OF FREEDOM OF EXPRESSION 665 (1970)

I dissent from the assumptions of the Conference Recommendations on Broadcast Journalism. I believe that regulatory procedures such as the Fairness Doctrine implement rather than offend the First Amendment since such procedures are designed to secure the first amendment interests in free debate and informed decision-making.

PART C

RECOMMENDATIONS
ACCESS TO GOVERNMENT
INFORMATION

XI

Government agencies should be required to respond to requests for access to public records within **10 to 20 days.**

(Unanimously adopted)

Commentary: One of the major problems with the operation of the Freedom of Information Act is the time that it takes to answer a request through the administrative process. It is not uncommon for an agency to take from two weeks to six months to act upon a request under the Freedom of Information Act. As a result, the Act has been, to a large extent, futile and unused by the news media, which needs information on a deadline basis. By setting a time period of 10 to 20 days, this problem would be resolved.[1]

---

1. Mr. Lightman commented that 10 to 20 days may be too long a period for the news media to wait for needed documents. He would like to see a 24 to 48 hour maximum response period.

XII

A Chief Public Information Officer should be placed in each government agency to be responsible for handling Freedom of Information Act matters.

(Narrowly Adopted)

Commentary: A Public Information Officer (PIO) is sensitive to the needs and interests of both citizens and the news media in connection with obtaining information from the agencies. However, some Conferees stated that the job of the PIO might be to make the agency look good in the eyes of the public and that a PIO would be reluctant to release information that showed the agency in an unfavorable light. Others believed that a PIO would restrict the flow of information in certain circumstances.

XIII

The Freedom of Information Act should apply to Congress.

(Adopted by substantial majority)

Commentary: If the Freedom of Information Act is to secure the people's right to know the actions of their government, this should extend to the legislative as well as the executive branch. Congress has attempted self-reform in connection with public access, but it is coming too slowly and in piecemeal fashion.

Some Conferees felt that legislators need confidentiality especially in mark-up sessions and in meetings with staff, and to make the Act apply to Congress would be to cut off some of the valuable internal discussions that take place.

XIV

The principles of the Freedom of Information Act should be extended to the states.

(Adopted unanimously)

Commentary: It was recognized that each state has different statutes and conditions governing access to state and local information. But information in the possession of state and local governments affects very closely the lives of the governed. Therefore, the Conferees felt that all states should adopt laws similar to the federal Freedom of Information Act so that the public will be informed about government actions at all levels.

XV

Courts should be permitted to assess the government for court costs including legal fees incurred by successful plaintiffs in taking Freedom of Information Act cases to court.

(Adopted by substantial majority)

Commentary: The public and members of the press, who are without great financial resources, have been unable to avail themselves of the judicial review provided by the Freedom of Information Act because of the high cost of legal fees. The costs can run more than $1,500 for even the simplest of cases. Public use of the Act would not normally result in financial gain and there are few individual citizens who can afford to bring a case under the Act under such circumstances. It was pointed out that only when an agency is subject to court review does it begin to comply with public access requirements in any meaningful way. Granting legal fees to a successful plaintiff was seen as a means of bringing more cases to court and thereby improving agency compliance. Paying legal fees also was seen as a penalty against agencies for wrongfully withholding documents.

XVI

Sections of government records which are the final work product of
a professional, should be a public record and should not be withheld
as an internal memorandum.

(Adopted by substantial majority)

Commentary: Under Section (b) (5) of the Freedom of Information Act
"interagency or intra-agency memoranda or letters which would not be available by
law to a party other than an agency in litigation with the agency" may be withheld
from public disclosure. Large numbers of government documents contain factual
information intertwined with opinions or recommendations and these documents —
usually in the nature of inter- or intra-agency memoranda — often are withheld
solely because of opinion content, not because of the facts.

When these documents are the end product of the work of a government
professional, the final written work should be a public record regardless of the
opinion content, thus making the public aware of the basis for government actions
and permitting a meaningful evaluation of government decisions.

XVII

(Note: The following are interrelated Recommendations.)

A. There should be special counsel, acceptable to the plaintiff, who
will meet security clearance qualifications of the government,
with the cost of clearance bourne by the government.

B. Any attorney may seek a security clearance without connection
to particular case so that the attorney may be able to participate
in any future *in camera* proceeding involving classified documents
while representing a plaintiff.

(Adopted by substantial majority)

Commentary: The obvious problems of allowing counsel to participate *in camera* is
that, if extremely sensitive documents are determined by the court to be properly

withheld, they should not be shown to persons not "cleared" to see them. To avoid this problem the Conferees adopted proposals to have attorneys "qualified" to participate in *in camera* inspection.

If special counsel is determined to be necessary, because of the government's argument that cases involving security information cannot be argued unless all participants are cleared for access to security information, the government should bear the cost of the clearance regardless of the outcome of the case.

XVIII

In order to withhold any part of any government document from the public, the government should justify the withholding of that part of the document, and should not merely assert that the specified document contains "secret" material.[1]

(Adopted by substantial majority)

Commentary: One of the greatest problems in government classification of and refusal to release documents is overclassification. Normally, whenever any document contains any reference, sentence, or phrase, deemed "secret" by the government the whole document is classified and any derivative documents which come from or refer to the original document receive the same classification as the initial document, even though they may not refer to the particular item which necessitated the classification. In this way, millions of documents which have no justification for classification, and significant portions of other documents which deserve only partial classification, are fully classified.

---

1. Mr. Weaver cites, in support of this Recommendation, the decision of Judge John Sirica, Jr. (8/29/73), In Re Subpoena Duces Tecum, the Cox-Nixon suit, 360 F. Supp.1 (D.D.C. 1973), on the severability of privileged and unprivileged material and the right of the Judicial rather than the Executive Branch to make the determination as to privilege.

XIX

The court system should have the following powers:

A. To exercise a *de novo* review under the Freedom of Information Act of the classification of records which are withheld from the public in the name of national defense or foreign policy.

B. To examine, *in camera*, the content of such documents to determine the propriety of classification.

C. To order the release of classified information when the classification is considered improper.

(Adopted by substantial majority)

Commentary: This Recommendation resulted from a discussion of the recent Supreme Court decision in *Environmental Protection Agency v. Mink*, 410 U.S. 73, (1973). In that decision the Court stated that, under the Freedom of Information Act, the district court could do no more than determine whether the document sought was classified by the agency pursuant to executive order. If an agency certified by affidavit that the document was in fact classified, the Supreme Court held that the district court's review could not review or assess the propriety of the classification. In reference to 5 USC 552 (b) (1), which permits withholding of matters that are specifically required by executive order to be kept secret in the interest of the national defense or foreign policy, Justice Stewart stated in his concurrence:

> ... it (Congress) has built into the Freedom of Information Act an exemption that provides no means to question an Executive decision to stamp a document 'secret', however cynical, myopic, or even corrupt that decision might have been. 410 U.S. 73 at 95.

The preceding Recommendation is an attempt to provide the courts with the means to review the decisions of agencies which withhold documents under Section (b) (1) of the Freedom of Information Act. Section (a) (3) of the Act directs that district courts determine cases *de novo* with the burden on the government agency to sustain its withholding. The Recommendation would clarify the Congressional intent to apply the court's *de novo* review powers to matters under Section (b) (1). The question was raised whether a district court judge is competent to review questions of major national and international importance. The Conferees determined that, even though there might be some difficulties with court review, it would be better than the present system of unchallengeable Executive power in withholding government records in the name of national defense or foreign policy. The district court in its review should be able to develop standards of what should be classified without having to rely solely upon the standards provided by the President in current Executive orders.

XX

Adversary counsel should be present at *in camera* proceedings.

(Adopted by substantial majority)

Commentary: This is necessary to protect the rights of plaintiffs to guarantee that the court receives full benefit of arguments from both parties. If counsel for plaintiff is not allowed to participate *in camera*, he can only argue abstract theories of law before the court since he will not know the contents of the documents that the court is reviewing.

The Conferees discussed the proposal that a review by the court of the documents should be exclusively *in camera*, without counsel, but with government representatives that the judge deems necessary.

The Conferees felt strongly that counsel for plaintiff should be permitted to participate in proceedings *in camera* so that he can adequately advocate the position of his client. The Conferees did not find it an acceptable alternative to have *in camera* inspection conducted by the court and any outside expert that the court may wish to include. To do so might tend to deprive the plaintiff's counsel from knowing all of the facts so he can fully advocate his client's position.[1]

---

1. Mr. Weaver stated: "In retrospect, probably reflecting considerable exposure to In Re Subpoena Duces Tecum, the Cox-Nixon suit, I think I would prefer *in camera* inspection by the judge alone, possibly with some sort of specially-qualified advisor. The presence of counsel, however cleared, seems to raise too many serious problems."

XXI

Specific intent to harm the nation's security should be retained as a basic element of the federal espionage laws.

(Adopted unanimously)

Commentary: U.S. Senate Bill 1400 (93rd Congress, First Session), an administration-sponsored recodification of the U.S. Criminal Code, would make release of classified information a criminal offense whether or not the releaser had intent to harm the United States or had reason to believe the release would be harmful. The Conference agreed that a person should be guilty of the crime of espionage *only* when specific intent to harm the nation, or reason to believe there would be harm, could be clearly shown.

The Conference agreed that the President should establish rules for protection of security information within the administrative structure of the Executive Branch but that the rules would have no force of law outside the Executive Branch. The Conference discussed and defeated a Recommendation on whether Congress should, by statute, establish a system for classification and protection of national security information to include penalites for overclassification and underclassification.

XXII

A government agency should be established by Congress, independent of the Executive Branch, to review national security documents and report to a congressional committee on the use and abuse of the classification system and on the operations of the Freedom of Information Act.

(Adopted overwhelmingly)

Commentary: This agency would function in much the same way as the General Accounting Office, being responsible to Congress but not acting as a super-agency whose judgments would be binding on Congress or the courts.

At present, there is no method of overseeing the system for classifying and protecting national security information, and the major implementation of the Freedom of Information Act covering non-classified documents is handled by the small staff of the Foreign Operations and Government Information Subcommittee.

JOURNALISTS' PRIVILEGE:
ONE YEAR AFTER BRANZBURG

by Benno C. Schmidt, Jr.
Professor of Law, Columbia University School of Law

1. Introduction

Each time I try to pull together my thoughts about reporters' privilege, I seem to alter my basic assumptions about sound policy.[1] Perhaps this flux is a concession to the lessons of experience and the process of trial and error, as Justice Brandeis urged was wise for the judicial function as well as the physical sciences;[2] but I fear my views may be more akin to Justice Roberts' characterization of a departure from precedent as a "restricted railroad ticket, good for this day and train only."[3] I am not confident that I can satisfactorily come to terms with the diverse social interests at stake in the question of journalists' privilege. At least there is evidence that I am not alone in my difficulty.

The Supreme Court has rejected a constitutionally-grounded immunity for reporters from compulsory process, but the decision was more tentative than many have thought and was carried by the thinnest majority. Then Congress embraced the question with an enthusiasm befitting a matter of well-publicized interest to the nation's news media. With uncharacteristic alacrity, bills were introduced and hearings got under way against a backdrop of vociferous and widespread commitment to reporters' privilege. As of this writing (June 1973) however, both Senate and House Subcommittees are having great difficulty achieving consensus on a draft bill to report to the full Judiciary Committees.

Paradoxically, the widespread interest in legislation to protect journalists' confidential information may be an impediment to enactment. Congress does not operate successfully as a town meeting, unless legislation affirms the commonplace or obscures complexities in vague formulations. All complex legislation on matters of general concern proceeds against strong centrifugal tendencies. The committee system usually counters this force by diminishing both responsibility for and interest in most statutes. But the widespread congressional interest in privilege legislation, coupled with the very substantial complexity of the subject, threatens to dissipate the strong overall commitment of Congress to protect journalists' confidential sources. Moreover, as proposals for absolute protection have given ground to the instinct to balance and qualify, the press is losing its enthusiasm for legislation, calling to mind Mark Twain's adage that the sensitive of stomach should not watch the making of laws or sausages. Senator Ervin, a less squeamish observer, recently remarked — in connection with his third quite different proposal — that the subject of reporters' privilege was the most difficult on which he had tried to formulate a statute in his nearly two decades as a Senator.

The question of journalists' privilege is now mainly a question of legislative policy in the hands of Congress. But congressional action will also have a major influence on further evolution of judicial doctrine concerning reporters' privilege, and not only in the obvious sense that the courts will be charged with interpreting any statute which eventuates. In dealing with this subject, I believe the Supreme Court is as much in dialog with Congress as it is grounded in the First Amendment. The interpretation of constitutional doctrine by the courts frequently proceeds not solely by reference to substantive constitutional principle but through interaction with the Legislative and Executive Branches which give great flexibility to the gradual evolution of constitutional doctrine.[4] The present Supreme Court has raised this sense of institutional interaction, always a significant undercurrent in the Court's jurisprudence, to a pragmatic well-spring of decision. So it is with the protection of reporters' confidential sources. Institutional responsibility for the development of the constitutional law of reporters' privilege is not compartmentalized. The Court and Congress are in the first stages of serial responsive readings. The Court will view the constitutional claims of journalists in the future in different perspective depending on whether and how Congress accepts the Court's invitation to deal with the matter by legislation.

Although the question of journalists' privilege to protect confidential sources of news from compulsory disclosure has been with us since colonial days, the problem has assumed major significance only in the last decade. We have seen increasing resort to subpoenas to ferret out confidential sources and information, and reciprocal defiance on the part of reporters to becoming evidentiary sources for official investigations.[5] Over the last decade, journalism and law have both struggled to accommodate traditional procedures and principles to the development of widespread disenchantment and disobedience in American society. Whether the cause has been the rights of racial minorities, resistance to the draft, protest against the war, or exploration of different levels of consciousness, many groups have advocated and often acted in disregard of the law. There is no denying the social importance of these alienated groups, and thus journalists have had to attend more than ever before to dissident groups whose activities are likely to be of interest to law enforcement agencies. The press itself reflects our society's fragmentation; "underground" newspapers and partisan organs devote themselves to the activities of alienated groups, while the mass media give considerable publicity to such activities.

Promises of confidentiality are a valuable resource in penetrating the suspicion and hostility of alienated groups. A journalist's efforts will be substantially impeded if his subjects feel that anything he learns will become available to those social institutions to which they are opposed. While journalists always have made use of promises of confidentiality in probing beneath the surface of press handouts, outright lies, and self-serving secrecy, my impression is that the use of confidentiality in digging out important stories is now more extensive than ever. Certainly, to the extent that the practice is necessary for coverage of disenchanted groups in our society, it has greater social value than ever before. Whatever disagreements we might have about dealing with alienation and disenchantment are academic until we have access to information. Without extensive press coverage of underground groups and cultures, we are left the skeptical but uninformed captives of the self-interested statements of the groups themselves,

or of the equally-inflated rhetoric of official spokesmen charged with their investigation and control.

At the same time that the political and cultural fragmentation of our society has led to new uses for reporters' promises of confidentiality, official corruption, bureaucratic infighting, secrecy and dissimulation at various levels of government — all of which traditionally have been the impetus for much confidential information being passed to journalists — show no evidence of recession. On the contrary, we seem to be in full flush of a second gilded age, where venality is challenged only by vicious zealotry as a stimulus for criminal malfeasance by secretive and sanctimonious officials. The deluge of confidential information from every part of the Executive Branch now threatens to swamp the most avid reader. Watergate is the triumphant symbol of investigative reporting from confidential sources and has already led to a fundamental shift in the outward attitude of officialdom toward the press.

Functional developments within the media have also contributed to the tendency of journalists to collect confidential information, which might be of interest to law enforcement authorities. As electronic media have become the source of most people's information about immediate, clear-cut events, print media have turned increasingly to perspective studies and investigative reporting. In the process, print journalists have adopted sophisticated investigative techniques, including extensive use of confidential informers.

Finally, changes in official attitudes seem to have led to the increased use of subpoenas against members of the press. Law enforcement and investigative agencies have been progressively strained in coping with the magnitude of their responsibilities. A journalist who has accumulated evidence of official corruption or probed the activities of militant radicals must seem a tempting investigative aid to these pressured officials. Moreover, we have indisputable evidence of growing official antagonism to the values which underlie the First Amendment. Concerned journalists see in the increased use of subpoenas a technique to harass the press and to emasculate its efforts at uncovering facts that officialdom would prefer to remain unpublicized.

2. The Branzburg Decision

The Supreme Court took notice of the importance of the problem in granting *certiorari* in three typical instances where newsmen had refused to divulge information received in confidence. Since the Court's response to these cases is now a year old, it may be well to review briefly the facts and the opinions of the Court.

In one case, a staff reporter for the *Louisville Courier – Journal* wrote two stories describing activities he had witnessed by invitation of drug users and sellers in and around Louisville. He was subpoenaed to appear before a state grand jury to testify about possible violations of state laws prohibiting the sale and use of drugs.

The second case involved a television newsman for a New Bedford, Massachusetts television station, assigned to report on civil disorders in New Bedford during the summer of 1970. Sent to cover a Black Panther news conference, he was allowed to remain inside the Panther headquarters in New Bedford to cover a raid by the police which the Panthers expected. However, the Panthers had required, as a condition of entry, that the newsman agree not to disclose anything he saw or heard inside the headquarters, other than the anticipated police raid. He stayed there for about three hours, but the police did not raid, and the newsman submitted no report on what transpired in the headquarters. Two months later, a state grand jury investigating the disorders called the newsman and asked what he had seen in and around the Panther headquarters.

The best known of the three cases involved Earl Caldwell, a black reporter for *The New York Times* assigned to investigate and report on the activities of the Black Panthers in Oakland and San Francisco. Caldwell conducted and taped several interviews with Black Panther leaders, and wrote several articles in the *Times* about the Panthers' positions and activities. Caldwell was subpoenaed to appear before a federal grand jury to testify "concerning the aims, purposes, and activities of that organization."

Each of these newsmen resisted the subpoena on first amendment grounds, but their position was rejected by the Supreme Court.[6] The majority of the closely-divided Court, in an opinion authored by Justice White, viewed the compelled testimony in these cases simply as "incidental burdening of the press" resulting from enforcement of civil or criminal statutes of general applicability. The reporters had sought a testimonial special privilege on the basis that otherwise the flow of information from news sources preferring to remain confidential would be significantly diminished. Justice White responded that the actual extent to which reporters needed to promise confidentiality was not clear. Not all news sources insist on confidentiality, he pointed out, and most reporters are not compelled to testify even when they have received information in confidence. Moreover, the opinion speculated, informants who have insisted on confidentiality often have a substantial interest in dissemination of news which would outweigh any fear of investigation. Thus, the fear of substantial drying up of news sources was doubted. But, Justice White argued, even if some constriction in the flow of news should occur, the public interest in investigating and prosecuting crimes reported to the press should predominate.

A substantial factor in the majority's skepticism toward a journalist's privilege rested on practical and theoretical difficulties. The reporters urged that the government be required to meet three tests before compelling disclosure of confidential sources of information: (1) that there is probable cause to believe that the reporter possesses information relevant to a specific violation of law; (2) that the information sought cannot be obtained by alternative means for sources other than the reporter; and (3) that there is compelling and overriding governmental interest in the information.

The majority opinion responded that the third of these tests would require the courts to make a purely legislative policy choice. Government presumably has a compelling interest in information about the violation of any and all of its criminal laws; courts are not in a position to weigh the value of enforcing different criminal laws so as to choose which are important enough to justify investigation into a reporter's confidential information. Justice White also argued that acceptance of a reporter's privilege would lead to confusion in determining who qualified for the privilege — a troublesome problem in light of the traditional doctrine that the liberty of the press extends to the village scold as well as professional journalists. Moreover, whether there is probable cause to believe a crime has been committed, or whether the reporter has useful information which the grand jury cannot obtain elsewhere, were felt by the majority to pose extremely difficult determinations for courts to resolve.

After seemingly rejecting both the theoretical and the empirical arguments for a journalist's privilege, the majority opinion concluded with an enigmatic suggestion that the door to the privilege may not be completely closed. "Newsgathering," the majority noted obliquely, "is not without its first amendment protection":

[G]rand jury investigations if instituted or conducted other than in good faith, would pose wholly different issues for resolution under the First Amendment. Official harassment of the press undertaken not for purposes of law enforcement but to disrupt a reporter's relationship with his news sources would have no justification. Grand juries are subject to judicial control and subpoenas to motions to quash. We do not expect courts will forget that grand juries must operate within the limits of the First Amendment as well as the Fifth.[7]

The majority's whisper of encouragement was echoed, if not clarified, in a brief but potentially important concurring opinion of Justice Powell. He emphasized "the limited nature" of the Court's upholding, and stated that "we do not hold that ... state and federal authorities are free to 'annex' the news media as 'an investigative arm of government'." No "harassment" of newsmen will be tolerated, Justice Powell continued, if a reporter can show that the grand jury investigation is "not being conducted in good faith" or if he is called upon for information "bearing only a remote and tenuous relationship to the subject of the investigation." Moreover, judicial relief could be forthcoming if the reporter "has some other reason to believe that his testimony implicates confidential source relationships without a legitimate need of law enforcement."

Thus, Justice Powell seems to recognize that a journalist has an important interest in protecting confidential sources, but for him the legal context is critical to balancing this interest against society's vital interest in law enforcement. He would demand a concrete record of particular questions about a specific confidential relationship before attempting to reconcile the reporter's first amendment claim and society's interest in detection and prosecution of crime. In a footnote, he reminds us that Caldwell asserted a privilege not even to appear before the grand jury unless the Government met his three preconditions. Justice Powell rejects this notion that the State's authority should be thus tested at the threshold. Instead, he seems to suggest that the balance can better be drawn when actual questions are asked and the reporter refuses to answer. Presumably, Justice Powell agreed with the decision reached in the other two cases because, although questions were actually put, the reporters in those cases rested their right of refusal on an absolute journalists' privilege rather than on an ad hoc demonstration that the particular questions were improper. Justice Powell evidently believes that, in constitutional terms, not all grand jury questions are the same, not all journalists are the same, not all confidential relationships are the same, and (perhaps) not all crimes are the same. Relevant differences, in his view, can be gauged only when the issue is at a riper stage than in Caldwell where the reporter had failed even to appear, or than in the other two cases, where the reporters rested their noncompliance on an absolute claim of privilege. If my reading of his opinion is correct, Justice Powell in a future case may join the four dissenters in upholding a journalist's claim that the First Amendment justifies a refusal to disclose confidential information.

Four justices dissented. Justice Douglas expressed his own categorical view and Justice Stewart wrote a more balanced opinion for himself and Justices Brennan and Marshall. For Justice Douglas, the proper decision is a simple reflection of his absolute view of the First Amendment: "There is no 'compelling need' that can be shown which qualifies the reporter's immunity from appearing or testifying before a grand jury, unless the reporter is implicated in a crime." He characterized as "amazing" the Times' position that the journalists' privilege should be balanced against competing needs of the Government. If Justice Douglas' first amendment privilege is taken in conjunction with his view of the privilege against self-incrimination, I suppose a reporter need never answer anything.

Justice Stewart wrote a careful but impassioned dissent. His starting point was the broad right to publish guaranteed in our society by the First Amendment, from which he deducted a corollary right to gather news. This right, in turn, requires protection of confidential sources "as a matter of simple logic once three factual predicates are recognized": 1) newsmen require informants in gathering news; 2) confidentiality is essential to creation and maintenance of a newsgathering relationship with informants; and 3) unbridled subpoena power will deter both informants from divulging sensitive information and reporters from publishing it.

The journalists' privilege which Justice Stewart would protect is not absolute. The interest of the Government in investigating crime is substantial and Justice Stewart believes it can properly outweigh the journalists' privilege if the Government can show: 1) that the information sought is "clearly relevant to a precisely-defined subject of governmental inquiry"; 2) that the reporter probably has the relevant information; and 3) that there is no other available source for the information.

What conclusion, then, can be drawn about the future of journalists' privilege in the courts? Despite what might appear at first to be the Court's flat rejection of the privilege, I believe a working majority rejected the view that journalists can claim no special protection under the First Amendment but should be treated like any person with knowledge of illegal activity. Justice Powell's concurrence reflects at the very least an open mind about extending to newsmen a qualified privilege to refuse testimony that would jeopardize confidential relationships. Moreover, the Court's judgment does not in any respect suggest limitation on the power of Congress to legislate a journalist's privilege. Indeed, the majority invited legislative consideration of the question:

> At the federal level, Congress has freedom to determine whether a statutory newsman's privilege is necessary and desirable and to fashion standards and rules as narrow or broad as deemed necessary to deal with the evil discerned and, equally important, to refashion those rules as experience from time to time may dictate.[8]

The Court's judgment in *Branzburg* is to some extent a holding action. A majority obviously feels that legislation is preferable to constitutional rule-making as the legal mechanism for reconciling the undeniable first amendment interest in protecting reporters' confidential sources taking into account society's interest in not clogging up fact-finding processes so as to impede law enforcement and other important official investigative functions. The majority was obviously concerned with the problems of line-drawing — particularly with respect to

who should qualify for the privilege — which it felt could be better handled by legislation. But my guess is that if legislation is not forthcoming from Congress, we will not have heard the last word from the Supreme Court on journalists' privilege. Indeed, some lower courts have already begun the process of limiting the scope of the *Branzburg* holding. The Second Circuit Court of Appeals has upheld on first amendment grounds a reporter's refusal to divulge a confidential source at the behest of a civil rights class action plaintiff. The Court regarded the *Branzburg* decision as limited to grand jury subpoenas, and concluded that civil judicial proceedings did not present a similar "rare overriding and compelling interest" which should overcome the first amendment value of protecting confidentiality. *Baker v. F. & F. Investment*, Docket No. 72-1413 (decided December 7, 1972).

The Prospects for Legislation
a. Is Legislation Needed?

The need for a statutory privilege is difficult to demonstrate because the facts concerning journalists' reliance on confidential information and the adverse impact of actual or threatened subpoenas are to a large degree speculative. Indisputable empirical data on these matters will in the nature of things never be available; the more extreme protestations of journalists and prosecutors must both be taken with a grain of salt.

The only careful empirical investigation as yet undertaken suggests that promises of confidentiality are frequently utilized by many journalists. Professor Vincent Blasi of Michigan Law School surveyed 975 working journalists from all media with respect to a variety of questions about press subpoenas. The newsmen in the survey reported average reliance on confidential sources for about one-quarter to one-third of all stories, with heavier reliance on confidential sources among more experienced reporters.[9]

Not surprisingly, stories about government operations involved the heaviest use of confidential sources, with something over one-third of the stories affected.[10] The medium which made greatest use of confidential sources was newsweeklies, affecting between one-third and one-half of the stories.

As for the adverse impact of actual or threatened subpoenas, Professor Blasi found that about eight per cent of his respondents reported that their coverage of a particular story within the past 18 months had been adversely affected by the possibility of subpoena. His findings, however, do suggest that the recent surge of press subpoenas "has generated widespread fears among reporters that their sources will 'dry up'."[11] Blasi's findings on this point, it should be emphasized, were collected prior to the Supreme Court's decision. Blasi found journalists virtually unanimous that nothing would have a more detrimental impact on source relationships than an adverse decision in the *Caldwell* case. The Supreme Court's decision has doubtless increased the difficulty of acquiring confidential information, as a result of the attendant publicity and imprimatur of the Court, and reporters would now presumably be even more negative about the impact of subpoenas.

While journalistic and social trends make a strong case in favor of a statutory journalists' privilege, it is equally the case that general trends in the law of evidence are moving in the opposite direction.[12] In light of this overall tendency away from privilege in the law of evidence, it is not surprising that the Supreme Court rejected a journalists' privilege resting on constitutional interpretation and judicial rule-making. As McCormick put it twenty years ago, "The development of judge-made privileges halted a century ago. The manifest destiny of evidence law is a progressive lowering of the barriers of truth."[13] Since evidence law is increasingly unsympathetic to privileges, and even the traditional attorney-client and interspousal privileges are regarded as dubious exceptions, Congress must look directly to the specific policy questions raised by a journalists' privilege, and not attempt to reason by analogy to traditional evidentiary privilege. Even if analogies could be drawn, their force as justifications would still be questioned by the many judges and practitioners who view the traditional privileges with skepticism.

The considerations Congress must weigh are the adverse impact of the present subpoena threat upon the flow of useful information to the public, as compared with the impediments to official investigations which different statutory privileges would create. If Congress concludes that one of these interests, as a general matter, substantially outweighs the other, then its response should be either to legislate sweeping privilege or to provide no

statutory protection whatever. If, on the other hand, Congress should conclude that both interests are substantial and worthy of recognition, it should attempt by statute to reconcile the two interests in some fashion, by protecting each interest when it is most compelling, while allowing it to be overcome when it is relatively less in jeopardy. Failure to enact any statute is to leave the official investigative interest dominant as a matter of law in all circumstances; the public interest in maximum dissemination of news is left to the discretion of prosecuting and other investigative officials.

It would be tedious to recite arguments that both the fullest dissemination of news to the public and official investigative processes with the means to get at relevant evidence are among the most important values in our legal system. I do not find it easy to assert that either one of these interests, stated at large and in the abstract, should overwhelm each and every particular human situation where the other interest is at stake. Would we want a reporter to be free from compulsion to disclose knowledge received under a promise of confidentiality of a plan to assassinate the police commissioner? I cannot find enough sustenance in the abstraction of freedom of the press to move me to such an unhumanitarian result. It is no answer to respond that any decent journalist would make such information known to the proper authorities. We do not trust to the compunction of ordinary citizens in obliging them to disclose evidence about such matters, and there is little reason to suppose that reporters are more mindful of their responsibility to support law enforcement than the rest of us. Reporters may, in fact, have strong professional interests in not jeopardizing source relationships by voluntary disclosure. The Blasi study found that a significant proportion of journalists would not give information voluntarily to officials in comparable hypothetical circumstances.[14]

Yet, I would not be happy if the Administration could put reporters under official compulsion to identify the sources of leaks, who were alleged to have violated the espionage statutes or other laws by revelation of "national security" information. For me, the definition of a reporters' privilege is a Burkian dilemma of drawing "balances between differences of good" with "political reasons [as] a computing principle." I agree with Professor Bickel that "[t]here is no clear First Amendment answer. There is only an unruly accommodation."[15] What, then, are the problems on which a journalists' privilege statute must reach an accommodation between the values of full dissemination of news and the interest of investigative processes?

b. Constitutional Questions

We can quickly dispense with constitutional issues. The commerce clause empowers Congress to enact a privilege operative against the states as well as federal investigative processes. It is well established in legislative and judicial precedents that institutions engaged in the dissemination of information to the public are engaged in "commerce among the several States," and are accordingly subject to broad congressional regulation and protection under Article 1, Section 7 and the Necessary and Proper Clause.[16] The objection that the commerce clause should not be utilized except for economic objectives, narrowly conceived, has no constitutional force. Since the turn of the century, Congress has, with judicial approval, used its power to regulate interstate commerce to effectuate broad notions of morality, social justice and the public interest. The Civil Rights Act of 1964, outlawing racial discrimination in places of public accommodation, is probably the best known recent instance of this use of the commerce power.[17]

A different sort of constitutional question about Congress' power to legislate a journalists' privilege concerns whether any guarantees of the First and Fifth Amendments impose definitional requirements, which would undermine the inevitable classifications which legislation would draw. In *Branzburg*, Mr. Justice White's opinion for the majority rejected the arguments for a privilege, in part because of what he saw as potential difficulties of definition and application:

> The administration of a constitutional newsman's privilege would present practical and conceptual difficulties of a high order. Sooner or later, it would be necessary to define those categories of newsmen who qualified for the privilege, a questionable procedure in light of the traditional doctrine that liberty of the press is the right of the lonely pamphleteer who uses carbon paper or a mimeograph just

> as much as of the large metropolitan publisher who utilizes the latest photocomposition methods . . . . The informative function asserted by representatives of the organized press in the present cases is also performed by lecturers, political pollsters, novelists, academic researchers, and dramatists. Almost any author may quite accurately assert that he is contributing to the flow of information to the public, that he relies on confidential sources of information, and that these sources will be silenced if he is forced to make disclosures before a grand jury.[18]

Despite Mr. Justice White's rather clear invitation for legislation, some have concluded from his catalog of the difficulties of limiting a journalist's privilege that the Supreme Court might not be hospitable to legislation, which would necessarily have to draw some of these lines. I believe such fears misunderstand the Court's rationale. Mr. Justice White was speaking of the difficulty of administering "a *constitutional* newsman's privilege," that is, one promulgated by the judiciary, under the constraints of principled adjudication. The problem which Mr. Justice White saw in the creation of a journalist's privilege is that which constitutional lawyers have termed the "under-inclusive classification": Will not others than those granted the privilege plausibly claim the appropriateness of being similarly treated? Such an argument is a powerful one when directed to the courts in the application of a constitutional mandate; "neutrality" of principle is surely essential to proper judicial action. But such a requirement of consistency is not imposed on the legislative process.[19] Courts have traditionally tolerated a piecemeal legislative approach to general problems and this latitude is not restricted to old cases or to economic or social regulations not deemed to involve civil liberties. *Katzenbach v. Morgan*, the leading modern decision dealing with Congress' power to legislate in aid of the individual liberties guaranteed by the Fourteenth Amendment, expressly approved an under-inclusive classification.[20]

This is not to say that Congress is free of constitutional restraints in deciding who should be given the benefit of a journalist's privilege. Congress may not legislate protection in a manner which discriminates among journalists or the media on the basis of content. In several recent decisions involving picketing in public places, the Supreme Court has reaffirmed that the equal protection clause prevents Government from imposing special restraints or affording special benefits to expression because of its subject matter. [21] Accordingly, size of circulation or longevity of employment relationships with the media are examples of standards which should not be used in legislating a privilege because they would tend to exclude, for example, the "underground" press.

On the other hand, Congress may insist on such elements as a current employment relationship with some medium of communication characterized by periodic publication, or a past record of publication in periodic media. These considerations are akin to neutral regulations of "time, place, and manner" which consistently survive equal protection challenge in statutes bearing on activities protected by the First Amendment. Thus, Congress is free to decide that, among the large category of reporters, novelists, scholars, teachers, and pamphleteers who could plausibly assert some claim to the privilege, certain occupational groups have an especially pressing need if the flow of information to the public is to be protected in its most significant, or vulnerable, aspects. There may indeed be much practical justification for such an approach where legislation moves into an area for the first time. [22] Whether a piecemeal approach would represent the better part of legislative wisdom in this instance is another matter, but I do not believe a narrow statute would find difficult sledding in the courts. No constitutional barriers exist to limit Congress' reasonable discretion in drawing lines which would qualify the privilege by limiting it to those classes of persons whom Congress regards as most in need of legislative protection in the interest of full and unfettered dissemination of news to the public.

c. Should a Federal Statute Bind the States?

Assuming the need for some statutory protection, the first major question of policy for Congress is whether both the federal government and the states should be bound by whatever privilege is enacted. Recent events suggest that the primary need for a journalist's privilege exists at the state level, although a statute would serve some important objectives at the federal level as well.

In August 1970, in response to strong press reaction to numerous Justice Department subpoenas to journalists such as Earl Caldwell, the Attorney General issued guidelines designed to reconcile the legitimate interests of the press and of federal law enforcement. These guidelines provide that no subpoena will issue without prior negotiation with the affected member of the press, and if negotiation fails, then only with the express authorization of the Attorney General. The standards for the Attorney General's approval require: 1) there be sufficient evidence of a crime from non-press sources ("the Department does not approve of utilizing the press as a springboard for investigations"); 2) the information sought must be "essensential to a successful investigation"; 3) the government must have unsuccessfully attempted to get the information from alternative non-press sources; 4) subpoenas should generally issue only to verify published information, and "great caution" should be exercised with respect to subpoenas for unpublished information or where confidentiality is alleged; 5) even subpoenas for published information should be "treated with care" because newsmen have encountered harassment on the grounds that information collected will be available to the Government; and 6) subpoenas should be directed to specific information.

As of last fall, in the two years the guidelines had been in effect, only seven subpoenas had been approved by the Attorney General. In congressional hearings last fall none of the spokesmen for privilege legislation could point to a single instance of subpoena abuse by the Justice Department since the guidelines. [23] At those hearings, the Justice Department opposed the passage of any qualified privilege as unnecessary in view of the guidelines. [24]

There are, nonetheless, two valuable purposes at the federal level which could be accomplished by legislation. First, the Attorney General's guidelines do not limit the issuance of subpoenas in connection with administrative or legislative investigations, or in private lawsuits. The "Selling of the Pentagon" controversy suggests the dangers of unnecessary subpoenas issuing from congressional committees, and administrative subpoenas are more numerous and potentially more damaging to journalists. Moreover, the Attorney General's guidelines, while a praiseworthy restriction of prosecutorial power, are subject to change at any time. And even if the guidelines remain in force, they lodge ultimate discretion in the Attorney General rather than providing, as a qualified statutory privilege would, for disinterested judicial review. The guidelines are necessarily flexible, and their administration could vary greatly depending on the sympathies of different Attorneys General. In sum, a statutory privilege at the federal level would add both scope and security to the protection of journalists from compulsory disclosures.

It is at the state level that recent events suggest the greater need lies. All but one of the recent publicized cases of actual or threatened incarceration of newsmen have been for refusing to disclose confidential information in the face of state investigative demands. While some twenty states now have some form of statutory privilege on the books, journalists in most states are without any protection. Moreover, even in states which have passed "shield" laws, judges have proved zealously adept at finding loopholes which allow reporters to be held in contempt, despite apparent statutory protection. William Farr's incarceration, for example, rested on the curious theory that, because he was not currently employed as a journalist when asked to identify his confidential source, he was not covered by the state shield law even though he was a regular journalist when he wrote the story.

The disruptive effect of state compulsions to testify is not limited to journalistic investigations and reporting only about matters of local interest. The communications media are of course nationwide. Even the most local news organs are reviewed by interstate media for information of general interest. Full disclosure of newsworthy matters of national significance may well depend on confidential information gathering, which could be hampered by state subpoenas. This is typically the case with respect to reporting about dissident groups or even certain kinds of local government misbehavior which may violate some federal statute or administrative regulation, or otherwise be of national interest. Given the wide sweep of basic state criminal jurisdiction, much confidential information about matters of national import may not be passed to journalists because of fears about state investigative processes.

Thus, I conclude that the basic federal interest in full dissemination of information of national signi-

ficance justifies a federal statute which limits state as well as federal subpoena powers. I recognize the value of local responsibility for law enforcement, but I believe the national interest in this situation justifies a statute of national applicability. The most significant state investigative interests can be taken into account in the qualifications which, in my view, should limit the force of any statutory privilege.

d. What Information Should be Privileged?

Protection of reporters' confidential source relationships should be the key element in defining what information comes within a statutory newsmen's privilege. Protection of the identity of sources will contribute — in some cases, at least, will be essential — to the willingness of sources to give information to the press, and the securing of newsworthy information that would otherwise be unavailable but which rests in the public interest in full news dissemination, justifying subordination of governmental investigative requirements.

On the other hand, an absolute protection for journalists from testimonial obligations is, in my opinion, not warranted. Reporters should of course be available to testify about all non-journalistic activities. No privilege should attach except for information received under a promise of confidentiality, and even though the privilege should not apply to information which has been published.

Where a journalist is an active participant in criminal activity, in the sense of aiding and abetting as opposed to mere observance, or where he engages in private activities relevant to civil litigation, no serious case can be made for a privilege. A harder case is where a journalist witnesses events in public in the course of journalistic investigations, such as the reporter assigned to observe a violent demonstration. Subjecting the newsman to compulsory disclosure in such a case may inhibit his capacity to cover similar events in the future, as is attested by recent incidents where newsworthy lawbreakers smashed cameras or otherwise prevented newsmen from recording information for fear that the records would be turned over to law enforcement authorities. Notwithstanding this kind of harassment, which has an adverse effect on the news-gathering capacity, no privilege should attach to information witnessed in public, where no element of confidentiality is present. The investigative value of reporters' eyewitness testimony will generally be high. And while reporters' capacity to cover public events can be subject to harassment, such actions, in the nature of things, will rarely cause coverage to be completely suppressed. The obligation to testify about public events, however, should not trench on confidential relationships, and therefore should not apply to situations from which the reporter could have been excluded:

> ... a newsman would have to testify as to his observations of demonstrations on city streets, but would not be required to disclose information relating to a meeting of a dissident group which could have excluded him from the meeting and which admitted him only because he promised to keep the proceedings off-the-record. [25]

The essence of a statutory privilege should be protection of confidential source relationships, and all confidential information should be treated as equally worthy of protection. The main distinction sometimes made here is between the identity of confidential sources and the information which they impart. Professor Blasi found that more than 90% of the reporters surveyed believed protection of identity was more important than protection of contents. [26] However, virtually all the reporters felt that both categories of confidential knowledge should be privileged if investigative reporting was not to be disrupted. While the identity of sources may be the most sensitive confidence in the hands of a reporter, the contents of confidential information could often provide investigative leads to the source.

In addition to protection of confidential source relationships, a separate and difficult question is whether, in general, reporters should be protected from subpoenas *duces tecum* to produce notes, tapes, films, photographs, first drafts, etc. Here the issues do not relate to the protection of sources, and consequent enhancement of availability of information to the public, but rather to the journalist's interests, and that of his medium in being able to make editorial decisions free of governmental scrutiny or second-guessing. Likewise, the issues on the prosecutor's side relate not to undisclosed information so much as to the probative force of tangible evidence as against testimony by the reporter. The required production of notes, tapes, or first drafts is more directly in conflict with freedom of the press than compelled testimony in that the quality of the actual article, report, or newstape disseminated to the public is more directly affected. If journalists' stock in trade can be as freely compelled as testimony, then journalists will be constrained in the initial writing, filming, or taping, when freedom and flexibility are most necessary. Otherwise, the quality of the final product will suffer. I, therefore, see a greater threat to the First Amendment in subpoenas requiring production of tangible work product, and would strike the balance more on this side of journalists' privilege than with respect to testimony.

e. Scope of the Privilege

Many of the bills aimed at protecting confidential relationships introduced in the last session of Congress contained exceptions for investigations of great public importance. For example, S. 3932 qualified the privilege if an official "demonstrated a compelling and overriding national interest in the information." Other proposals were more specific. S. 1311, for example, lifted the privilege if a court determined "that there is substantial evidence that disclosure of the information is required to prevent a threat to human life, espionage, or foreign aggression." In addition, some bills would lift the privilege from allegedly defamatory information received in confidence, where the defendant in a civil action for defamation asserts a defense based on the source of such information.

Carefully-defined exceptions to a journalist's privilege to deal with situations of special investigative urgency seem to me justifiable, so long as the information sought by the investigator is not available from alternative sources. Under no circumstances should a reporter be compelled to breach a confidence where the investigative need could be satisfied by evidence from a different source.

A general subjective exception, in the manner of S. 3932, however, seems unsatisfactory in imposing on the courts an obligation to decide an amorphous question without guidelines. When a similar argument was made in the *Branzburg* case that such a judicial responsibility was implicit in the First Amendment, Mr. Justice White responded for the Court:

> ... by considering whether enforcement of a particular law served a 'compelling' governmental interest, the courts would be inextricably involved in distinguishing between the value of enforcing different criminal laws. By requiring testimony from a reporter in investigations involving some crimes but not in others, they would be making a value judgment that a legislature had declined to make, since in each case the criminal law involved would represent a considered legislative judgment, not constitutionally suspect, of what conduct is liable to criminal prosecution. [27]

As for more specific statutory exceptions to the privilege, I agree with the Second Circuit in the *Baker* case that civil cases do not present a justifiable occasion for lifting a statutory privilege. Criminal investigations, on the other hand, do present situations where I would override a statutory privilege. Prevention of foreign aggression and espionage are obvious overriding concerns, at least if the legislation makes clear that the latter is limited to the usual conception of clandestine transmission of information to foreign agents and not public dissemination through the publication of government secrets. Investigation of a threat to human life also is a compelling basis for overriding the first amendment interest in protection of confidentiality, although I would require the threat be directed to specific (even though not necessarily identified by name) lives, to prevent the privilege from being overriden whenever an investigation can point to apocalyptic rhetoric of dissident groups.

The privilege should also be overcome in the interest of solving past crimes of a particularly serious nature. Investigation of murder seems an appropriate exception to a statutory privilege. Other crimes involving egregious risks of death, such as arson of an occupied building, skyjacking, or kidnapping might be appropriate exceptions to a statutory privilege, even when no death has resulted. Additional crimes of extreme seriousness might be added to the excepted list, but obviously the value of the privilege in first amendment terms will be diminished if the list is unduly enlarged. Each situation considered for an exception should present a strong social justification for unimpeded investigation. Exceptions must be limited and sufficiently definite to avoid the creation of loopholes which would erode the privilege.

In the area of crimes of governmental corruption or malfeasance, on the other hand, where journalism based on confidential sources has frequently served as the most effective means of exposure, the privilege is essential to the public interest, and no exceptions for criminal investigations should be created.

The appropriate scope of a journalist's privilege at the trial stage of criminal proceedings poses problems of exceeding difficulty. The right of a criminal defendant to compulsory process for obtaining witnesses in his favor is of constitutional dimension under the Sixth Amendment, reflecting the paramount value we attach to protecting innocent persons from conviction. While the interest of the prosecutor in fullest access to testimony at criminal trials is not of constitutional dimension, it is nonetheless of the highest social importance. In proving guilt beyond a reasonable doubt, the prosecutor may, in unusual but conceivable circumstances, have need to negate exculpatory hypotheses by evidence not obtainable except by breaching a journalist's privilege. In such a situation, the prosecutor's interest in overcoming the privilege at trial would be more compelling than his interest in calling the newsman before the grand jury in similar circumstances, in light of the much stricter burden of proof on the prosecutor at trial. Thus, compulsory process at criminal trials — whether in behalf of the prosecution or the defense — should overcome the journalists' privilege, so long as the instigating party can satisfy the condition (which should apply to all exceptions to the privilege) that there is no available alternative source for the same evidence.

f. To Whom Should the Privilege Extend?

The most troubling question concerning a journalists' privilege for confidential source relationships is who should be able to claim its protection. The Supreme Court, as we have seen, regarded this issue as posing serious constitutional problems for a judicial privilege grounded in the First Amendment. While Congress is not similarly hedged in by constitutional difficulties in determining to whom a statutory privilege should extend, the basic question of legislative policy nonetheless remains.

Obviously, the statutory privilege should cover anyone regularly employed in a newsgathering or disseminating capacity by any newspaper, wire service, periodical, broadcasting station or network. Free-lance professional journalists should also be covered, provided their professional status is established by a showing of prior publication or broadcast of their materials in one of the covered media. Congress should go further than a regular employment relation or prior experience and protect anyone clearly associated with an established medium of communication, in connection with the journalistic story for which he claims the privilege. This would include free-lancers who, though not having the professional experience referred to above, could demonstrate some tangible connection with a medium of news dissemination. Potential journalists, working without a contract on their first stories, would not be covered, but this gap in the protection of some confidential sources seems well worth the administrative convenience and protection of investigatory powers inherent in having some definite limits on the reach of the privilege.

A vexing problem is what should be considered a medium of news dissemination, for purposes of establishing an employment relation or other connection. Professor Blasi has suggested that one requirement for such a medium be some element of periodicity — "continuing publication [including broadcasting] at more-or-less regular intervals." This would prevent witnesses from altering their immediate behavior to achieve statutory protection. Such a requirement might exclude the upstart publication, but again the cost seems worth the gain of providing relatively clear limits on the reach of the privilege.

Extending a statute to cover all free-lancers, authors, scholars, lecturers, pamphleteers, etc. would reflect first amendment values that are somewhat less weighty than the value of protecting dissemination by regular journalists. Moreover, extending a statute to cover such categories would introduce very difficult problems of administration. The initial legislation should enter this sensitive area cautiously, leaving open the possibility of broadening the reach of the privilege at a later date in the light of further experience.

Notes to
JOURNALISTS' PRIVILEGE:
ONE YEAR AFTER BRANZBURG
by Benno C. Schmidt, Jr.

1. I have tried to write about this subject twice before, once immediately after the Supreme Court's decision, Schmidt, *Beyond the Caldwell Decision*, Columbia Journalism Review, Sept.-Oct. 1972, p. 25, and the second in a statement submitted to Congress on behalf of the Association of the Bar of the City of New York. See 28 Record of N.Y.C. B.A. 308 (1973). I have borrowed liberally from these earlier statements for portions of this paper.

2. *Burnett v. Coronado Oil and Gas Co.*, 285 U.S. 393, 408 (1932).

3. *Smith v. Allwright*, 321 U.S. 649, 669 (1944).

4. See generally Bickel, *The Least Dangerous Branch*, 260-68 (1962).

5. A useful catalogue of recent subpoena cases is reported in Graham and Landau, *The Federal Shield Law We Need*, Columbia Journalism Review, March-April 1973, pp. 26, 30.

6. *Branzburg v. Hayes*, 408 U.S. 665 (1972).

7. Ibid. at 706.

8. Loc. cit.

9. Blasi, *Press Subpoenas: An Empirical and Legal Analysis*, (1972), p. 22.

10. Ibid. at 26.

11. Ibid. at 41.

12. In this modern tendency, evidence law may be thought to reflect the restrictive views of Professor Wigmore towards all privileges:
There must be good reason, plainly shown, for their existence. In the interest of developing scientifically the details of the various recognized privileges, judges and lawyers are apt to forget this exceptional nature. The presumption against their extension is not observed in spirit. The trend of the day is to expand them as if they were large and fundamental principles, worthy of pursuit into the remotest analogies. This attitude is an unwholesome one. The investigation of truth and the en-

forcement of testimonial duty demand the restriction, not the expansion, of these privileges. They should be recognized only within the narrowest limits required by principle. Every step beyond these limits helps to provide, without any real necessity, an obstacle to the administration of justice.
Wigmore, 8 *Evidence* Sec. 2192.3.

In this spirit, the proposed Federal Rules of Evidence restrict existing privileges and make no provision for a journalists' privilege. See Rules 501 *et seq.*

13. McCormick, *Evidence* Sec. 85.

14. Blasi, *op. cit.* at 31 *et seq.*

15. Bickel, *The Press and Government: Adversaries Without Absolution*, Freedom At Issue, May-June, 1973, pp. 5, 6.

16. Licensing of local radio and television stations under the Communications Act of 1934 is based on the constitutional premise that all persons engaged in public broadcasting are engaged in or affect interstate commerce. 47 U.S.C. Sec. 301. As for print media, the Newspaper Preservation Act of 1970 exempts certain activities of local newspapers from federal antitrust regulation, which is only applicable to activities in interstate commerce, in the "public interest of maintaining a newspaper press editorially and reportorially independent and competitive in all parts of the United States." 15 U.S.C. Sec. 1801. Moreover, instances are numerous where general regulatory statutes applicable only to activities in or affecting interstate commerce, such as labor or anti-trust laws have been upheld as applied to newspapers, magazines, wire services, and broadcasters. See, *e.g.*, *Mabee v. White Plains Publishing Co.*, 327 U.S. 178 (1946); *Lorain Journal Co. v. United States*, 342 U.S. 143 (1951).

17. 42 U.S.C. 2000a; see *Heart of Atlanta Motel, Inc. v. United States*, 379 U.S. 241 (1964).

18. *Branzburg v. Hayes* at 703-05.

19. "[A] statute aimed at what is deemed an evil, and hitting it presumably where experience shows it to be most felt, is not to be upset by thinking up and enumerating other instances to which it might have been applied equally well, so far as the court can see." *Keokee Consolidated Coke Co. v. Taylor*, 234 U.S. 224, 227 (1914).

20. 384 U.S. 641 (1966). The court upheld legislation eliminating English literacy requirements for non-English speaking citizens educated in American-flag schools where English was not the primary language, a statute which in practice enfranchised only persons educated in Puerto Rico. The statute was challenged because it did not grant relief to other citizens educated in Spanish-speaking schools which did not happen to fly the American flag. Even though the source of congressional power to enact the provisions was the Equal Protection Clause of the Fourteenth Amendment, where one might expect to have found implicit the most stringent requirement of legislative consistency, the Supreme Court affirmed traditional principles of legislative flexibility:

. . in deciding the constitutional propriety of the limitations in such a reform measure we are guided by the familiar principles that . . . 'reform may take one step at a time, addressing itself to the phase of the problem which seems most acute to the legislative mind.'
Ibid. at 657.

21. See *e.g.*, *Police Dept. of Chicago v. Mosley*, 92 S. Ct. 2286 (1972).

22. Tussman and tenBroek, *The Equal Protection of the Laws* SELECTED ESSAYS ON CONSTITUTIONAL LAW, p. 795 (West, 1963):

The 'piecemeal' approach to a general problem, permitted by under-inclusive classifications, appears justified when it is considered that legislation dealing with such problems is usually an experimental matter. It is impossible to tell how successful a particular approach may be, what evasions might develop, what new evils might be generated in the attempt to treat the old. Administrative expedients must be forged and tested. Legislators, recognizing these factors, may wish to proceed cautiously, and courts must allow them to do so.

23. See Hearings before Subcommittee No. 3 of the House Judiciary Committee on Newsmen's Privilege, 92nd Cong., 2d Sess. (1972).

24. Ibid. at 21 Statement of Assistant Attorney General Roger Cramton.

25. Note, *Reporters and Their Sources*, 80 Yale L.J. 317, 368 (1970).

26. Blasi, *supra* at 63.

27. *Branzburg v. Hayes* at 705-06.

THE FIRST AMENDMENT AND
BROADCAST JOURNALISM

by Professor Sig Mickelson
Professor of Journalism
The Medill School of Journalism
Northwestern University

Broadcasting is such a volatile business and memories are so short that it is probable that few persons now remember a cause celebre of the 1950's.

It was an event in which broadcasting's relationship to the First Amendment received a solid buffeting; an event in which a major setback could have been suffered. No specific conclusions were reached as a result of the curious storm that raged for several weeks. No landmark precedents were established but, in a sense it was a watershed since it cleared the air and at least negatively established that broadcast journalism couldn't be throttled at the whim of an irritated government.

The event was a special "Face the Nation" program produced by CBS News and featuring Nikita Khrushchev, the First Secretary of the Russian Communist Party, as the guest.

The program was filmed at the Kremlin in Moscow. Ground rules agreed on with the Soviet leadership were relatively open. The format was essentially the same that the show still follows except for the fact that an interpreter intervened

---

Professor Mickelson was First President of CBS News.

between guest and panel. The First Secretary was vigorous, ebullient and responsive to questions. It was in this program that he uttered what has now become a famous phrase, "We will bury you."

The program was broadcast on a late Sunday afternoon of May,1957, at a time when television as a force in news and public affairs coverage was still in its experimental infancy. There were no warnings at the time of an impending storm. The next morning the Khrushchev interview was the headline story over the entire country: *The New York Times*, the *New York Herald-Tribune*, and the *Washington Post* ran the full text. It was clearly the most newsworthy effort performed thus far by television.

By Monday afternoon proof was at hand. It was unmistakably evident that the Secretary of State, John Foster Dulles, was outraged by the network's effrontery in furnishing an outlet for a national appearance by the leader of the country's principal enemy. The President was said to be upset. Critics on the right who had not fully recovered from the McCarthy period started cannonading CBS by telegram, letter, telephone call and messages to their congressmen.

CBS absorbed the early shock with confidence but then it began to waiver. On the Tuesday morning after the Sunday program, I was summoned to the twentieth floor CBS Board Room at 485 Madison Avenue immediately on arrival at my office. The meeting, which began almost at once, carried on throughout that entire day and well into the next day. The participants included CBS News' Public Affairs Director, Irving Gitlin, and Director of News, John Day. From the corporate executive staff there were Frank Stanton and Richard Salant, who later succeeded me as President of the News Division. News Division personnel couldn't see any problem arising out of the special Khrushchev "Face the Nation" program; only clear advantages to CBS. Corporate management saw it differently. They anticipated a genuine threat to CBS' freedom to cover the news and, what is worse, believed that the interview might have given impetus or might in the future give impetus to the passage of restrictive legislation in Congress. Of course, there always was that overriding fear that something might be done to the licenses of the five CBS-owned television stations, which constituted a principal source of net revenue to the corporation.

It took the arrival of an outside public relations counsel to resolve the dilemma. He encouraged the adoption of an affirmative position rather than a negative one. He urged CBS to take the offensive; show pride in "Face the Nation" rather than embarrassment; brag to the country about having made a major contribution to better world understanding rather than apologize for having given the Russian leader an opportunity to speak directly to the American people.

Even more significantly the CBS response — reflected in full page ads in the New York and Washington newspapers on the next morning — became the springboard for a campaign on behalf of broadcasters' freedom of the press that was to last for several months. The campaign demanded first amendment protection for broadcasting.

Whether anything specific was gained as a result of this campaign, at least nothing was lost. More importantly, broadcasters were set on a course that would lead to increasing claims on the first amendment protection, as complete as that claimed by the printed press.

Since that occasion, the First Amendment has become a rallying point for defenses by broadcasters against all manner of criticism. First amendment defenses have been triggered by causes ranging from the closing off of news sources, the issuing of subpoenas to reporters for appearances and subpoenas to editors for out-takes, to more general material with less obvious immediate results including various applications of the "Fairness Doctrine."

In fact, there is some reason to think that the "First Amendment" phrase may have been worked so hard that it has begun to lose its meaning. Some broadcasters tend to use the words "First Amendment" much as the Israelites used trumpets at the Battle of Jericho. Recite the words "First Amendment" seven times and the barriers to full protection will collapse, permitting broadcasters to walk unchallenged into the inner sanctum so long occupied exclusively by the printed press.

The matter is not nearly so uncomplicated. It is true that the Federal Communications Act of 1934 seems to promise a "hands-off" attitude on the part of government toward broadcast program content. Included in that Act is the paragraph which reads:

> Nothing in this Act shall be understood or construed to give the Commission the power of censorship over radio communication or signals transmitted by any radio station and no regulation or condition shall be promulgated or fixed by the Commission which shall interfere with the right of free speech.

There is only one exception to this affirmation that broadcasters shall have the right of free speech and that is found in the Federal Criminal Code which specifies that fines up to $10,000 can be assessed for use of "obscene, indecent or profane language." The Criminal Code also forbids broadcast of information about "any lottery, gift enterprise or similar scheme." This would seem to give broadcasters reasonably clear sailing insofar as their news policies are concerned. But the actual record of performance of government in its relationship with broadcasting suggests that other considerations frequently take precedence over this apparently clear and incontrovertible statement.

There are two facets of the Federal Communications Commission's (FCC) regulation of broadcasting which permit, at least by indirection, an abridgement of the freedoms which seem to be so clearly guaranteed. The first of these arises out of the licensing procedures and the second is from the "Fairness Clause" in Section 315, which did not become a part of the Communications Act until 1959.

The licensing procedure itself is sufficiently complicated and, therefore, vulnerable to a variety of abuses. Since there is no way of designing a fool-proof scale on which to judge competing applications, the commissioners must rely on fallible and subjective human judgments.

The procedure becomes vastly more complicated when taken in context with the great variety of new elements added by the application and growth of the "Fairness Doctrine." The "Fairness Doctrine" itself added a sufficiently complex new element but, when it was not only affirmed but somewhat convoluted by the *Red Lion* decision in 1969, the opportunity for utilization of the licensing procedure for the imposition of a philosophy became vastly strengthened.

It's a curious fact in the development of broadcasting in the United States that what passes for progress has frequently been nothing more than a series of trade-offs. When broadcasters were given the right to editorialize in 1949, they were obligated to follow a "Fairness" rule. They were quite willing to live with "Fairness" as it applied to editorials but found that it tended to be inhibiting when applied to straight news broadcasts and documentaries, which exhibited any genuine courage in attacking community problems.

In 1959 broadcasters succeeded in softening the "Equal Time" clause of Section 315. They were granted the right to cover candidate appearances in regularly-scheduled news broadcasts, news interviews and news documentaries without being forced to yield equal time. Here, too, there was a trade-off. For this privilege they gave up any claim they might have had to the elimination or weakening of the "Fairness" clause. It was written into the law and was no longer a simple statement of FCC policy. And the increasing complexity of interpretations, growing like barnacles on a ship's hull, added new and complex dimensions.

The *Banzhaf* cigarette case in 1966 extended the application of the "Fairness Doctrine" to commercials. This move was reinforced by the *Friends of the Earth* case. In the midst of this gradual extension of the application of the "Fairness Doctrine" came the *Red Lion* decision, handed down by the Supreme Court in 1969.

It's odd how an innocuous little sentence, which simply specified that broadcasters have the obligation to "afford reasonable opportunities for the discussion of conflicting views on issues of public importance," could be stretched to the point where it could be applied to almost any part of the broadcasting schedule. The *Red Lion* case really didn't add any new elements; it only shifted the focus. No longer could a broadcaster assume that following the good journalist's rule of objectivity would insure compliance. The Court shifted the emphasis from the rights of the media to the rights of the listener-viewer to hear and see a diversity of voices, attitudes and ideas. Thus was born the controversy over "public access," a controversy which has been raging since the *Red Lion* case and shows no promise of abating.

The problem with the application of the "Fairness Doctrine" is that, once you expand the list of criteria and apply a set of standards no matter how vague they may be, it is necessary for human judgment to be applied to determine whether performance measures up to standards. The standards themselves must necessarily have been set as a matter of human judgment.

"Ascertainment" is a logical by-product of the strict application of the "Fairness Doctrine" as it relates to measurement of station performance. A station manager is under obligation to ascertain the needs, interests and desires of his community and to build a program schedule which caters to those needs, interests and desires. If his license comes under challenge he must prove that his "ascertainment" procedures were thorough and sound and that his program schedule recognizes all the factors discovered in his ascertainment exercise.

All of this sounds very logical and quite innocuous. Obviously the trustee of a public award of a frequency to communicate should perform in the "public interest, convenience and necessity." But unfortunately, there are no hard and fixed guidelines on which to judge his performance; no scientific units of measurement that can be applied; no objective devices available for judging.

It is the subjective nature of this process that frightens broadcasters when a Vice President on a speaking platform in Des Moines, Iowa, or the Director of the Office of Telecommunications Policy in Indianapolis, Indiana, lays down criticism of "elitist gossip" and "ideological plugola." If his locally-generated news programming or that obtained from the network is to be judged on the basis of political prejudice couched in scare words, he has a just reason to fear that his position is insecure.

If intemperate criticism comes from officials holding high office, the fears can be intensified. The gradual erosion of the defenses implied in the censorship phrase in the 1934 Act is small comfort. No wonder he worries whether his license may be at stake if he broadcasts any matter which might be regarded as critical of those in power.

The Chairman of the Federal Communications Commission, Dean Burch, conceded at a hearing of the Sub-committee on Communications of the Senate Commerce Committee in February that there are dangerous elements in the "Fairness Doctrine." Senator Pastore asked him the question: "We're getting into the area of censorship here, aren't we?" Burch's answer: "I'm afraid that the 'Fairness Doctrine' by definition comes a little close to the area of censorship in the sense that we require certain things to be put on the air."

The trouble with "Fairness" is that it has broad parameters. If "Fairness" were simply construed as a requirement to maintain the news tradition for objectivity and balance, enforcement would be a relatively simple matter. Most broadcasters are dedicated to objectivity anyway and the extremists who have no interest in maintaining it could be quickly identified.

When "Fairness" is projected into national political affairs or the elections, it becomes more complicated. A network has an almost impossible position in trying to keep some reasonable balance between the party in power and the out-party. The American system does not lend itself to the easy identification of the logical spokesman for the loyal opposition. The "Equal Time" provision takes care of the appearances of candidates during election campaigns but "Fairness" is a much more subtle thing and subject to a vast range of interpretations.

CBS' ill-fated attempt to set up a mechanism for giving an opportunity to the loyal opposition, to be heard in a program entitled "The Loyal Opposition" in the summer of 1970, illustrates the difficulty involved in trying to work out an institutionalized system for performing the role. CBS furnished the Democratic National Committee a half hour of time to respond to a number of presidential speeches. Party Chairman Lawrence O'Brien, rather than answer precisely the points made by the President in his preceding half hour message, ranged broadly over a number of issues in which he flayed the Republican Party vigorously. The Republicans asked for time to answer. The Federal Communications Commission decided that they were, under the terms of the "Fairness Doctrine," entitled to such time. CBS did the only thing it could do: It put the program in mothballs and hasn't been heard from since.

I walked headlong into a very carefully constructed trap eight days before the 1958 election. On a Sunday afternoon I received a call asking whether I was interested in giving live coverage to a meeting of President Eisenhower's Cabinet, scheduled to take place the next day. I replied in the affirmative, provided it would be a genuine Cabinet meeting with all members present. My theory was that the public had never seen the inside of the Cabinet Room, had never seen the Cabinet members assembled with the President and that they had no idea as to the procedures followed in regular Cabinet meetings. This seemed to be an eminently useful first in the television business and so I took the next step which was to call Jim Hagerty, President Eisenhower's press secretary at the White House, to discuss the offer more fully with him.

Hagerty told me that he could schedule the Cabinet meeting at our convenience on the next day, a Monday. We decided on a one-hour period between 7:00 and 8:00 p.m. Affiliated stations were quickly informed of the decision, a mobile unit and crews were assigned to start setting up first thing next morning and the special events director in Washington was given the responsibility of handling all the logistical details.

Hagerty was as good as his word. Secretary of State Dulles failed to appear because he was on one of his many trips, but the other members of the Cabinet were all on the scene. The President called on them, one by one, to make reports. The cameras were placed in advantageous positions to get both the members of the Cabinet delivering their reports and the reaction of the President. Response to the program suggested that the public was interested and grateful for the opportunity to see an American institution, about which they had read many times, in action.

It was equally obvious, however, that this Cabinet meeting was staged. The purpose was not to conduct the normal business of the United States; it was not to discuss serious issues and arrive at honest conclusions. The purpose was to display the President and the Cabinet of the United States, Republicans all, to voters of both parties, just eight days before a national election. I had unwittingly given the Republican Party one hour of free time on the CBS radio and television networks in the guise of its being an event of public importance.

For this error CBS could surely have been charged with violation of the "Fairness Doctrine," unless it were to make amends by furnishing the Democratic Party with a similar hour at some reasonable time before the election. The Democrats complained about the so-called "Cabinet Meeting." They described it as a trick, which it surely was, but they did not demand time to answer. The Democrats became the winners of the election and apparently no damage was done, except to my own standards. Since those days "Fairness," however, has become a much more complicated commodity.

Turning to the *Banzhaf* cigarette case, Mr. Banzhaf was able to convince the Federal Communications Commission that since cigarette smoking — which is potentially injurious to the health — was a matter of public interest and concern. He further argued that the "Fairness Doctrine" demanded that messages calling attention to the possible damaging effects were urgently required. The Commission agreed and a new interpretation of "Fairness" had been written into the history of the Communications Act. Under this new interpretation not only news and public affairs programs were subject to "Fairness" interpretations, but also commercial advertising.

Many broadcasters had long followed a policy of refusing to sell time for the discussion of controversial issues, but sometimes the policy had been breached. CBS television for a number of years had permitted the electric light and power companies to broadcast commercials in connection with the "You Are There" television programs, which were obviously designed to sell the virtues of private utility systems. Network and corporate officials eventually, however, discovered the error and insisted that the commercials sell products and not ideas. The advertising was duly changed to conform.

David Wolper, the Hollywood producer of documentaries and feature films, came into my office one day in 1958 with a one-hour documentary program relating to man's effort to conquer space. The program was entitled "The Race for Space." I

screened it with Wolper, found it thoroughly researched, skillfully produced and about as entertaining as a documentary program could be, but I turned it down. The basis for the decision was that the protagonist in the program which placed heavy emphasis on the efforts of the U.S. Army to develop a space program was General Medaris, the head of the Army space program. It so happened that at this point in history the Army, the Navy and the Air Force were engaged in a vigorous battle to see which of the three services would gain command of the country's entire space program. As it turned out none of the three did. The responsibility was ultimately given to the National Aeronautics and Space Administration (NASA). But carrying that program at that particular time with its strong Army bias and its glorification of General Medaris would certainly have been unfair to the other two services and, in a sense, to the Administration as well, since it was undoubtedly preparing even at that early stage to award the plum to NASA.

Our decision, later supported by both ABC and NBC, turned out to be an unalloyed boon for Mr. Wolper. He took his program to the Music Corporation of America, built an independent network for it, engendered a groundswell of favorable response and was off to a highly-successful career in film production. CBS was undamaged. It retained its self-respect and pride and, as a matter of fact, produced a vastly better show in the "CBS Reports" series. However, the "Fairness Doctrine" was beginning to close in. We were criticized in the most vigorous way for keeping the network to ourselves, for not permitting divergent voices to be heard, for not permitting the development of new talents, for closing off the channels of access for persons outside the narrowly-limited sphere of broadcasting.

Public access has surely become the battleground for more criticism of the present structure of broadcasting than any single issue. In the 1940's the center of controversy was the "Blue Book," an FCC report recommending certain principles with respect to radio programming; in the 1950's among other things the Quiz Scandals commanded the major share of attention; the 1960's brought Civil Rights and the coverage of dissident elements in our society. Now, in the 1970's, the dominant theme is "Public Access."

"Access" has become almost as overworked a word in the language as "relevant" was in the late

'60's and "meaningful" before that. Not only is it overworked, it is so loosely used as to obscure its real meaning and its method of application to the broadcast scene.

What kind of access are we speaking of? Obviously we must include diverse opinions, ideas, attitudes. Obviously, opportunity must be granted to a diversity of groups, who now have little opportunity to be seen or heard, or to have their opinions seen or heard, on the established broadcast communications facilities.

However, providing such "public access" invites a great number of knotty problems.

Should the broadcast facility become a speakers' corner where all dissident or dispossessed groups have the opportunity to ascend the soap box and speak to the fulfillment of their utmost desires?

Should the role of the gate-keeper be transformed so that the gate-keeper becomes more a traffic policeman, regulating the flow of diverse persons, groups and ideas, than the executive charged with responsibility for policy formulation? Which serves the public interest better: A system in which management, responsive to a diversity of public interest, needs and desires, consciously establishes a policy and a mechanism to implement it, where the ultimate responsibility for the selection of the diverse ideas, attitudes, and opinions rest with him, or one in which the initiatives lie with groups seeking to utilize his facility for "public access" purposes?

Should groups with adequate financial resources be permitted to purchase blocks of time to carry their points of view to the public? Or, should broadcasters be permitted to impose "flat bans" against the sale of time for the discussion of controversial issues?

Should access be achieved on the basis of direct contact between individual and station management, or should it be indirect access achieved through participation in advisory councils?

Could access requirements be solved through more careful attention to a diversity of voices and views in regular news and documentary programs, or must they be achieved through new and special efforts?

Will attention to a diversity of voices lead to fragmentation and chaos, or to a sounder approach to national problems since more ideas have been aired, more alternatives explored, more dissident voices brought into the formulation of policy?

Should more efforts to open access to communications media be supported in the interest of catharsis, or so that the nation will be better able to formulate sound policy by broadening the inputs?

Most importantly, does the "right to speak" serve as a sufficient guarantee of first amendment rights, or should there be some concomitant "right to be heard" in order to carry out fully the mandate of the *Red Lion* case? Groups or individuals using "public access" are likely to be shocked by the paucity of viewers or listeners to their performances unless they are integrated into existing programming.

The cumulative effect of the *Banzhaf, Friends of the Earth*, and *Red Lion* decisions seem to have established, as a matter of public policy, an obligation on the part of broadcasters to furnish "public access." The *Business Executives Move for Peace-Democratic National Committee* case is still to be heard from but the decision most likely will relate only to part of the problem — the question of "paid access" as opposed to "free access."

The matter of furnishing such access is a complicated one. Carried to its ultimate end we would be creating a new "Tower of Babel," in which the cacaphony produced by a multitude of voices would leave nothing but chaos, confusion and frustration. At the same time a legitimate question can be asked as to whether freedom to use the air waves serves a more real purpose than simply giving the speaker an opportunity to blow off steam. If so, is it worthwhile devoting a segment of an enormously valuable public franchise for the purpose? We run the real risk, unless public access questions are settled judiciously and with restraint, of creating so many opportunities, giving them to so many varied petitioners representing so many diverse sources that we will be guilty of an "idea and opinion overkill." As a matter of fact, some think that we are being subjected now to an excessive volume of diversity.

Broadcast licensees are already committed to furnishing the type of diversity that is described in the *Red Lion* case and in the "Fairness Doctrine." Questions regarding how it should be carried out, however, are worthy of careful consideration.

It is self-evident that a license holder should be more than a traffic policeman. He obviously must know his community. "Ascertainment," even though the word has the tinge of government jargon, is a necessary requirement for understanding the problems and people of a community. The crucial question is whether the broadcast licensee can meet the requirements of "diversity" through his normal broadcast schedule and on a voluntary basis, or whether he must yield some control to outside, non-professional, special pleaders.

This country has had reasonable success in the past by entrusting the control of its media to a corps of professionals. For the most part these professionals have acted with wisdom and sensitivity for the public's welfare. A voluntary commitment to fairness, balance and objectivity has provided a bench mark to guide their decision-making.

On the other hand, there are distinct dangers involved both in too rigid an application of requirements for "public access" and in too broad an extension of the "Fairness Doctrine."

One danger arises from the fact that the broadcasting station could become an oriental bazaar, dedicated to the hawking of strange and exotic ideas, scheduled with no editorial judgment, no selectivity and no guaranteed relevance to current problems.

It is entirely likely that an uncontrolled or lightly controlled public access system could be monopolized by the more aggressive and articulate elements in society, which are neither the needy ones nor those with the most to contribute. The microphones and cameras could go to those with the greatest resources, the loudest voices, the most demanding attitudes and, in some cases, possibly the most frightening threats.

Counter-advertising, a linear descendant of the "Fairness Doctrine" and the *Red Lion* case, sounds like a completely reasonable theory. If detergents foul up sewer systems, why shouldn't ecology-minded groups have the opportunity to present messages countering advertising for the detergents? If gasolines pollute the air and contribute toward the onset of disease and eventual choking of cities, why shouldn't opponents have an opportunity to express a contrary point of view? If the construction of the Alaskan pipeline will damage the ecological development of the territory through which it passes, why shouldn't attention be called to this fact?

There are a number of distinct fallacies in this type of reasoning. In the first place, in the cases cited above, counter-advertising wasn't necessary to stimulate an intensive discussion of the issues. A national debate was generated without the aid of counter-advertising. However, more importantly, while little that is affirmative can be accomplished (note that cigarette consumption is higher now than it was when radio and television stations carried cigarette commercials), serious damage can be wrought to the economy of the broadcasting business. There is no point in arguing here whether economic strength is desirable. The fact is that our economy is governed by a profit motive. Until there is a better method of operating our communications media, it seems reasonable that we should do what we can to keep it economically viable. We can always switch to a public broadcasting system although the recent controversies over the Corporation for Public Broadcasting suggest that we haven't done too well yet in that area.

A greater concern stems from the fact that, as we broaden the application of the Federal Communications Act of 1934 by rulings, policy statements, amendments, court decisions and interpretations, we increase the number of entry points for government interference or intimidation and move further away from the theoretical protections of the broadcaster once thought offered by the First Amendment. It is true that broadcasters have been far too timid in the past. They have been much too inclined to tremble in terror at governmental criticism. They have been much too quick to fly the white flag for fear of government penalties. We should understand that there is a vast array of opportunities open to the government official for exacting punishment of one kind or another. Anticipation of punishment is frequently a sufficient threat to force a licensee to invest many hours of manpower and many thousands of dollars in building defenses. Encouragement of a competing application for his license, or hints of impending legislation serve as subtle constraints on his freedom to operate. Many of these fears are doubtlessly exaggerated, but a government license offers little defense if a government is determined to exact penalties or force compliance with a specific point of view, even though the First Amendment exists as a theoretical bulwark against government encroachment.

In short, there is nothing wrong with the principle of a "Fairness Doctrine" provided it is fairly imposed and is not used as a vehicle for broadening government controls over all phases of broadcasting. The definitions, so far furnished by the courts, superficially appear reasonable.

There are three principal interpretations: 1) A broadcaster must give adequate coverage to public issues. 2) Coverage must be fair in that it accurately reflects opposing views. 3) Coverage must be afforded at the broadcaster's own expense, if sponsorship is unavailable. Any of these three interpretations could lead to excesses, but, if adopted as general statements of principle, no broadcaster should take exception.

A general requirement for operating in the "public interest, convenience and necessity" assumes that the broadcaster will give adequate coverage to public issues.

A voluntary "Fairness Doctrine," which assumes that fairness is largely related to maintaining objectivity and balance, has previously ensured the broadcasting of a wide diversity of views, attitudes and opinions. And, with the addition of some creativity and ingenuity on the part of management, it could also succeed in presenting a diversity of faces.

The Cullman principle, the third of the interpretations listed above, is not unreasonable if it is employed only in significant cases. Where the controversy is of such demonstrated public concern that response is required as a matter of public policy and not of government whim, a non-paid response is probably in order.

The main dangers involving the "Fairness Doctrine" arise from the tendency of the Doctrine to encourage timidity on the part of broadcasters, the bracketing of "fairness" with "public access," and the decision in the *Red Lion* case.

The newly-refurbished "Fairness Doctrine" is thus more than a negative constraint disguised to maintain balance. It is becoming a positive force demanding that broadcasters take the initiative in seeking out voices, opinions and ideas which do not otherwise make themselves heard. If this is accomplished by voluntary "ascertainment" procedures, the broadcaster can't really object. It is to his advantage to know his community well for business as well as program reasons.

The danger is that he can be penalized for having missed some obscure element, and that his responsibility to follow up "ascertainment" can be judged on a set of standards that are subjectively established.

Maintaining objectivity is not a wholly mechanical procedure. Human judgment is required to measure the degree of objectivity or conversely of imbalance. But the human factor plays a greatly-enlarged role in assessing the sins of omission as opposed to the sins of commission.

An FCC commissioner would require the vision of a clairvoyant and the wisdom of a Solomon to determine who deserves to be heard and who to be overlooked. Additionally, his decision must be made without the benefit of living and working in the community in which the case arises.

It is no wonder that the application of the First Amendment to broadcasting becomes baffling. The Amendment protects the right of free speech but the government functionary decides how the broadcaster exercises it and who else in the community may have access to his facilities to use the privilege.

The Federal Communications Act prevents the Commission from exercising any power of censorship, but it can decide what is fair or unfair, and who has a right to use the facility to reply to management.

The Federal Communications Act specifies that "no regulation or condition shall be promulgated or fixed by the Commission which shall interfere with the right of free speech." Yet it can revoke a license if the broadcaster doesn't furnish diverse members of his community with the right to respond to his "free speech." Can speech really be free if it may result in license revocation? Of what value is the constitutional assurance if a single individual or a group of commissioners or the whole apparatus of government is in a position to make a subjective decision as to what is fair and unfair?

It is the response to this question that caused broadcasters to react so vigorously to criticism from the Vice President, the Director of the Office of Telecommunications Policy and other Administration officials in the period since the Vice President's Des Moines speech of November, 1969.

The vulnerability of broadcasting is predicated on the fact that it is difficult to separate content from other aspects of regulation. A drift from an assigned frequency can be judged objectively by mathematical calculations. Performance of service to the community furnishes no such mathematical scale.

Critics insist that broadcasting must be treated differently from the printed press because it uses a valuable and scarce commodity, the limited radio frequencies. It is true that the spectrum available for broadcast use is too limited to permit any applicant who wishes one to obtain a license but this doesn't necessarily furnish decisive proof that broadcasting is a dangerous monopoly. There are approximately 1,700 daily newspapers in the United States but there are 8,253 broadcasting stations. Of this total 922 are television stations, the remainder radio. Of the television licensees 701 are commercial.

The City of New York has three mass circulation daily newspapers. There are six commercial VHF television stations and one non-commercial.

Chicago has more mass circulation dailies than any other city in the country — four. But there are four commercial VHF television stations, three commercial UHF stations, one non-commercial VHF and one non-commercial UHF. In addition, there are more than 60 radio stations in Chicago and Cook County.

The limited spectrum is a serious constraint against obtaining a license to broadcast, but the investment costs required to go into newspaper publishing are equally onerous and serve as a very real obstacle, if not quite so obvious as that faced by broadcasting.

The scarcity of new metropolitan dailies starting up in the last three decades is testimony to the fact that the day of the pamphleteer with the mimeograph has long since gone.

It is true that there are only three national networks but there are likewise only three national weekly news magazines, two national wire services and two principal news syndication services. The networks may be a monopoly, but not quite as virulent a one as critics argue. Not enough for the imposition of restrictions that would chip away at the underlying philosophy of the American tradition for free dissemination of news and information.

Admittedly, there is a vital need for channels for the expression of a greater variety of ideas and opinions. There is a danger that our communications media might become so tradition bound and inwardly oriented that they would not be responsive to new thought or novel suggestion. There is the possibility that broadcast frequencies would be used, if all constraints were removed, for the maintenance of the status quo.

But we must weigh the advantages of free expression against a tightly-controlled system of public access, which could conceivably require more restriction and more interpretation in an evolving process of growing complexity in order to be workable.

At a recent conference at Ditchley Park in Oxfordshire, England, devoted to considering the relationship of broadcasting to media in eight countries with free election systems, there was widespread agreement that broadcasters should abide by a general self-imposed standard of fairness. There was concern, however, that fairness should not be so encrusted with detailed definitions, interpretations and requirements as to make it an objective in itself, rather it should be a broad-gauge guide to service to the listener-viewer. And the British delegate was particularly firm in pointing out that British broadcasting is fair without government rules.

Not all our broadcast deficiencies can be cured by a hands-off policy, nor can broadcasters rely wholly on the First Amendment to ward off criticism but our broadcast policies would be best served by giving the broadcaster freedom from the constraints imposed by Section 315, the ascertainment procedure and such other rules and policy statements as may open the door for influence of content. Perhaps in the future public access on the widespread scale, for which some broadcast critics now yearn, can be accomplished through cable. A broad-band communications system with 20 or 40 or even 60 or 80 channels will, in all probability, furnish ample opportunity to all who wish to use it, without conflicting with the interests of others. If we can wait until cable is ready to create an environment in which all voices can be heard and all ideas expressed before imposing restrictions which interfere with the basic rights of freedom of speech, we can maintain reasonable respect for the First Amendment.

In the interim, it is time for a thorough new look at the Federal Communications Act of 1934 and its instrument for the execution of government policy — the Federal Communications Commission. The Communications Act has been patched up, amended and expanded to cover new communications media and a myriad of new and unanticipated problems since its inception. Television was only a dream in 1934, radio in a primitive stage, and broad-band communications unheard of by lay persons. Communications satellites were something only for science fiction writers.

Radio news in 1934 was barely out of the pre-historic stage. Lowell Thomas, Boake Carter, and H. V. Kaltenborn were broadcasting news from network headquarters but the Associated Press was suing KSOO in Sioux Falls, South Dakota and KVOS in Bellingham, Washington for piracy of the news. A short-lived CBS News Service was organized in 1933 but was soon allowed to die quietly. Edward R. Murrow was in Europe hunting up speakers for the CBS "Talks" programs. Associated Press and United Press service to radio stations came later, as did the organization of network news departments.

In 1974, forty years will have passed since the Communications Act became law and the FCC organized, forty years of the most rapid changes in world history. The Communications Act like the Constitution may have been written for the ages but it is more likely to have been designed to meet a specific set of needs which existed in 1934.

The future is not likely to furnish breathing spells when we can pause to have a look at the whole communications regulatory structure. We shall have to do it on the fly. Therefore, it is appropriate to appoint a commission at an early date to examine the past 40 years of service, foresee the needs of the future, determine *not* where the Communications Act should be patched up but *whether* it should be retained, or a new structure established. Perhaps the impetus should come from a disinterested citizens group funded by non-profit agencies, rather than by an administration or congressional agency.

Broadcast communications have become so essential to the functioning of late Twentieth Century society that they deserve the best efforts of the most thoughtful people to make it possible for them to operate most effectively in the public interest. Special attention should be found toward developing mechanisms to keep them as free of government constraint as they can possibly be, consistent with the necessity of maintaining some type of licensing system. And regulations affecting content should be consigned to whatever final resting place accommodates all those old government laws, rules and agencies that have been found wanting.

ACCESS TO GOVERNMENT INFORMATION – THE RIGHT BEFORE FIRST AMENDMENT

by Samuel J. Archibald
Professor, Department of Communication
American University

Truth will become the hallmark of the Nixon Administration. I'm charged directly by the President to emphasize to every department of government that more facts should be made available. With this kind of emphasis, we feel that we will be able to eliminate any possibility of a credibility gap in this Administration.

This was the glowing promise presented in May, 1969 to the press and the public by Herbert G. Klein, the nation's first Director of Communications and one of the few apostles left in the White House after the Watergate Affair. It seemed, in the early months of the first Nixon Administration, that a large part of the promise might be achieved. Soon, however, it became apparent that the only major government information problem tackled was the credibility gap. But the credibility gap was not closed; instead, the Nixon Administration used the voice and the speechwriters of Vice President Spiro T. Agnew in an attempt to transfer the credibility gap to the press. What happened to truth as a hallmark of government, and to the hope that more facts would be made available by every department of government?

There was every chance that the public's right to know might be honored as never before when Richard M. Nixon took over the White House. He installed one of the nation's respected editors and his close personal and political friend as the government's first Director of Communications. Herb Klein had taken time off rom his editing job to help Richard Nixon in many of his earlier political trials.He had the ear of the President, he had his respect, and he also had the respect of the nation's press. Certainly, newsmen thought Herb Klein would be able to help Richard Nixon tear down the wall of bureaucratic secrecy that had grown tall as the Federal Government had grown huge.

In addition to his close relationship with the President, Herb Klein had another weapon when the Nixon Administration promised to join the battle against government secrecy. That weapon was the Freedom of Information Law, which had been in operation for only 18 months and had hardly been used in the dying months of Lyndon B. Johnson's administration.

The question is not whether Herb Klein made effective use of his weapons, nor even whether the Nixon Administration has come anywhere near its promise of open government. A few men clothed in the brief authority of government cannot guarantee a fully-informed public which is basic to the functioning of a democratic society. Nor can they prevent eventual disclosure of ineffective policy planning or sordid self-dealing in a nation of citizens who believe they have a right to know the facts of government — a right which precedes any first amendment prohibition against legislation abridging freedom of the press, which is but one part of the public's right to know.

The problem of a free flow of information is beyond any few men, any single administration of government. There may be no final solution in the complex world we have created. But we can consider some facets of the problem, and one of the more obvious facets is the availability of information from the Federal Government.

I

Once Congress passed a law abridging freedom of the press. The First Amendment to the Constitution prohibiting such legislation probably was quite fresh in the minds of those congressmen who voted for the law and of the President who approved it, for the law was one of the first acts of the First Congress. It was the "housekeeping" law of 1789, which merely authorized the head of every government department to prescribe regulations governing the custody, use, and preservation of the records, papers, and property of his department.

For nearly 160 years nobody realized that the housekeeping law (5 U.S.C. 22) permitted the federal bureaucracy to block press access to public records and that restrictions on press access were restrictions on press freedom. Dr. Harold L. Cross was hired as a legal advocate for the American Society of Newspaper Editors. He pointed out how the bureaucracy, in recent years, had twisted the housekeeping law into a claim of legal authority for secrecy.

The 85th Congress came up with a simple solution to the problem which the First Congress had unintentionally created. A sentence was added to the housekeeping statute stating, merely, that it did not authorize withholding information from the public.

In 1946 Congress had passed another law (5 U.S.C. 1002) which stated that matters of official record should be made available but added that an agency could hide its records "for good cause found" or "in the public interest." For those few bureaucrats who could not find good cause to show that secrecy cloaking their operations was in the public interest, the law provided another excuse. They were required to make the government records available only to persons properly and directly concerned.

In 1966 Congress put a dent in this shield of secrecy by passing what is generally known as the Freedom of Information Law. It did not solve the problems of public access to government information but it was a giant step toward legal recognition of the people's right to know.

The law (5 U.S.C. 522) states that any person — he need not be a person legitimately and properly concerned and need not even be a citizen — has the right of access to public records. It states that any person may go to court to enforce his right of access, and that the burden of proof is upon the government to prove that secrecy is necessary. Those are the important provisions of the Freedom of Information Law.

There are other provisions: requirements that agencies must publish and index all of their orders, opinions and other details showing their methods of doing business and a list of nine categories of public records which agencies may withhold. But six years of experience under the Freedom of Information Law have shown that the important provision is the right of the public to force the government to justify, in court, the need for secrecy.

Six years of experience also have shown that the government will not grind to a halt because of participation by the governed. The witnesses representing government agencies, testifying in opposition to the original bill, warned that it would. Every government witness argued that it would be impossible to operate the government if just anybody could come in off the streets and demand to see the records of public business. They even argued that interference with the right of the Executive to administer the laws would violate the Constitution.

II

With that kind of opposition, it would be unlikely if the government agencies followed the letter of the Freedom of Information Law, let alone administered it in the spirit in which it was passed by Congress. They didn't. Every agency was given a year to work out regulations implementing the law after it was signed on July 4, 1966. Most of the agencies waited until the Department of Justice put out a memorandum explaining the new law in the context of its legislative history, and the Department of Justice waited until nearly the last minute to complete its memorandum. The foreword by the Attorney General listed several key concerns Congress had in passing the law and the President in signing it:

- that disclosure be the general rule, not the exception;
- that all individuals have equal rights of access;
- that the burden be on the government to justify withholding, not on the person who requests a document;
- that individuals denied access have a right to take the government to court;
- that there be a change in government policy and attitude.

There was little change in government policy and no change in attitude toward the public's right to know. The text of the 47 page memorandum, which followed the Attorney General's introduction, gave many more excuses for withholding information under the new law than arguments for releasing it. The memorandum relied heavily upon the House of Representatives' report on the bill which became the Freedom of Information Law, and for good reason.

In two sessions of Congress before the final bill was passed, the U.S. Senate had passed similar legislation. The basic legislation had been drafted in the House of Representatives, where most of the

hearings exposing government secrecy had been held, and companion bills were introduced in the Senate. In the House, the legislation was referred to the Judiciary Committee since it amended the Administrative Procedure Act — the 1946 law which said information should be available unless an agency could find good cause, in the public interest, for withholding it. The hearings on government secrecy had been held, however, by a House Government Operations Subcommittee under Congressman John E. Moss of California. He and his subcommittee were deeply interested in legislation to protect the public's right to know; the Judiciary Committee was not nearly as interested, so each time the bill died in the House.

In the Senate, the investigations into government secrecy had been handled by a Judiciary Subcommittee headed, at various times, by Senator Hennings of Missouri, Senator Carroll of Colorado and, finally, Senator Long of Missouri. Thus, the companion bills introduced in the Senate to amend the Judiciary Committee's Administrative Procedure Act went sailing through the subcommittee. It is a fact of legislative life that a committee seldom makes changes in legislation approved by one of its subcommittees, and changes are even less likely in the full Senate. Thus, the legislation easily passed the Senate, but died in the House.

When the bill which finally was to become the Freedom of Information Law was referred to the House of Representatives, its opponents in the government agencies were sure it would die once more. This time, however, things were different because of some clever legislative maneuvering by Congressman Moss. His bill, identical to the Senate bill, did not amend the Administrative Procedure Act. It amended the old "housekeeping" law over which his subcommittee had jursidiction. Since hearings already had been held on his identical bill, Moss argued with the House leadership that the bill from the Senate should be referred to his subcommittee. It was, and the government agencies realized for the first time that there was a good chance Congress might actually pass a freedom of information law.

When the Senate bill went through the House subcommittee without change, there was a message to Moss from the White House. President Lyndon B. Johnson might try to block the bill in the House

Government Operations Committee (he had friends in high places on the Hill in 1966) unless the House report contained language that permitted the Department of Justice lawyers to write the kind of legislative history that would make them happy. The Department's lawyers worked with committee staff experts to develop that kind of language. The bill passed, the President signed it into law, and the Department of Justice put out an explanatory memorandum relying heavily on the language their lawyers helped write in the House report.

The Department of Justice memorandum was one step away from the ideal of a free flow of information, which had impelled Congress to pass the Freedom of Information Law. Regulations for all the agencies implementing the law were one more step away. In some instances, of course, the mere passage and implementation of the law made previously-hidden government records available to the public. This happened because top-level officials in government agencies were forced, for the first time, to take a hard look at their public information practices. Once they looked at the law and looked at their practices — and listened to those few agency lawyers who believed that the public really does have a right to know the facts about government — they ordered a change in some of their secret practices. There were not many, but there were a few — enough to justify Congressman Moss' belief that, if he could just get a good law passed, it would be the wedge needed to open locked file drawers filled with public records.

III

Was Congressman John Moss right? When he moved to another subcommittee, he was succeeded by Congressman William Moorhead of Pittsburgh, and Congressman Moorhead decided to find out.

Moorhead, like Moss, believed that the people really do have a right to know what their government is planning and doing. The Freedom of Information Law had been on the books five years when Congressman Moorhead mounted a major study of how it had been administered. His report stated that the operation of the law "has been hindered by five years of foot-dragging by the Federal bureaucracy." He also found that the foot-draggers could be convinced to move a lot

faster by the stimulation of a public hearing on their stewardship of public records. In addition, the Freedom of Information Law was not being administered by the government's information experts. He did learn that the courts were doing an excellent job of interpreting the law on the side of the public's right to know.

An analysis of the first four years of operation under the law, prepared for the Moorhead Subcommittee by the Library of Congress, disclosed that the law was being used by private interests to get public records for personal gain. That, of course, should shock no one who has gone beyond a high school civics textbook. People are human, and a workable democratic system of government must take account of their frailties as well as their strengths. A workable democratic system permits a clash of interests to be resolved, in the long run, for the welfare of the society which created the system. That is how the Freedom of Information Law seems to be working.

In the first four years of the Freedom of Information Law, two-thirds of the identifiable individuals or organizations using it to get public records have been profit-oriented corporations or law firms apparently representing private interests. Next in line — and way down the line — is the press, followed closely by public interest groups. The Library of Congress analysis prepared for Congressman Moorhead indicates that only one-tenth of the requests under the Freedom of Information Law were filed by the press, and slightly fewer were filed by public interest groups.

From a pragmatic view of government operations, this analysis is not surprising. To use the law effectively takes time — time to identify public records, time to file a written request, time to file an administrative appeal, time to go to court, if necessary. And each one of these steps which takes time also takes money.

The press does not have the time, for news is a perishable commodity. The press does not have the money, for routine government news does not sell newspapers nor draw television viewers. These same problems face public interest groups, but the press has an additional problem with the use of the Freedom of Information Law. A reporter's sources are his livelihood. He can push them just so hard. If he is too insistent or too demanding, the public

USERS OF 5 USC 552*
July 4, 1967 to July 4, 1971

Type of individual or organization refused access to public records:	Number of requests
Corporation	390
Private law firm	250
Media	90
Public Interest Law firm or group	85
Non-federal government agency	53
Researcher	41
Member or staff of Congress	34
Labor union	13
Other (unidentifiable individuals or organizations)	547

* Source: Hearings, March, 1972, Foreign Operations and Government Information Subcommittee, pp. 1340-1341.

record he seeks will be made available — to the opposition newspaper or broadcasting station.

Together with showing who has been using the Freedom of Information Law, the Library of Congress study of the first four years of the law's operation also indicates which of the nine exemptions government agencies have been using as reasons for secrecy. It is interesting to note that the fear, expressed repeatedly by government witnesses testifying against the then proposed law, would lay

**SECTIONS OF 5 USC 552 (b) (1) THROUGH (9) CITED BY AGENCIES
AS AUTHORITY TO REFUSE ACCESS TO PUBLIC RECORDS***
July 4, 1967 to July 4, 1971

Section of law	Number of instances all agencies have cited Section in refusing access
(1) national defense or foreign policy	30
(2) internal personnel rules	100
(3) exempted by other statutes	206
(4) trade secrets	403
(5) inter- or intra-agency memoranda	375
(6) invasion of personal privacy	344
(7) investigatory files	244
(8) financial institutions	7
(9) information concerning wells	11

* Source: Hearings, March, 1972, Foreign Operations and Government Information Subcommittee, pp. 1342-1343.

bare the nation's defense secrets, was not well-founded. It is not the secrecy surrounding military operations or international negotiations that is so dramatic; the rub is in the huge bulk of routine administrative secrecy.

Even more impressive is the record of the courts in handling complaints against improper secrecy in the first four years of the law's operation. Another study done for Congressman Moorhead by the Library of Congress analyzed the results of some 40 reported court cases, and indicated the trend in court decisions interpreting the nine exemptions of the Freedom of Information Law.

The study shows that the exemptions upon which the government relied most as explanations for secrecy were not holding up in court as valid reasons for withholding the information. In each of the six cases in which the government contended that a public record must be withheld because it contained "trade secrets and commercial or financial information obtained from a person and privileged or confidential," the courts rejected the government's argument. And the trade secrets' argument was the one most often used by government agencies as a claim of authority for withholding information.

The exemption of intra-agency or inter-agency letters or memoranda was a close second in government use, and the courts rejected the government's argument in 60 percent of the cases in this category.

In two other categories of exemption, the Library of Congress study reported, there had been enough court decisions to indicate a trend. Seven cases involving the exemption of investigatory files compiled for law enforcement purposes had been decided, and the courts ruled on the side of the government in all but one of the cases. Three cases involving information kept secret in the interest of national defense or foreign policy had been decided, and the government won all of these cases.

The Freedom of Information Law, it seemed, was working as its early supporters had hoped. The courts were exercising careful judgment and requiring the government to prove the need for secrecy. In the administrative grey areas of trade secrets and agency memoranda, which the government was using the most to claim authority for secrecy, the courts were denying the government authority. In the sensitive areas — investigations and national

security — the courts were supporting the need for secrecy. But that is only part of the picture.

In ten cases the government had argued that the court had no right to look at government documents and make an independent determination of whether the excuse for secrecy was justified. In seven of those cases, the court looked at the documents anyway. All of the three cases, in which the courts decided they had no authority to second-guess a government decision under the Freedom of Information Law, involved national defense or foreign policy exemption.

There is action underway to change all this. Hearings already have been held on a bill by Congressman Moorhead to permit the courts to look at classified documents, in camera if necessary, and decide whether the documents properly fall within the national defense and foreign policy exemption. The Moorhead Amendments would make other important improvements. They would require agencies to respond much faster to a request for public records — possibly within ten days — and would make an administrative decision on appeal within the same time limitation. The bill provides for reasonable court costs and attorneys fees if the government loses a freedom of information case. The provision to speed government action on request for information might make the law a more useful tool for the press. The provision for payment of legal costs might make it a more useful tool for individuals and organizations who cannot afford a long court battle.

Whether or not the Moorhead Amendments become law, a big hole has been torn in the paper curtain of secrecy surrounding the Federal Government, and it can be made bigger if the law is used more often.

Only 13 percent of government agency refusals to disclose public records requested under the Freedom of Information Law during its first four years were appealed to the head of the agency. The law does not set up an administrative appeal provision, but the Department of Justice memorandum recommended that final decisions on refusal be made by the head of an agency if the case may possibly go to court. While too few of the refusals are appealed, it seems to be an effective procedure since agency heads reversed their subordinates' decisions to withhold public records in nearly 29 percent of the cases.

The more the law is used, the more effective it will become. There is a good chance a citizen will win an administrative appeal against secrecy, and an even better chance he will win in court — in fact, government restrictions on public records were reversed, in whole or in part, in 57 percent of the court actions listed in the Library of Congress study.

IV

There are many facets to the government information problem. There is, for example, both a negative and a positive side. The negative excuses for withholding information from the public in a democratic society are no more important than the system set up for a positive flow of facts — not propaganda — from government agencies. The negative and positive sides of the flow of government information each have their own problems which often tend to overshadow the major issue.

One of these problems is information classified as "Top Secret," "Secret" or "Confidential" in the name of national security, a problem which has been around as long as the idea of national sovereignty but which has been approached under a classification system only since 1940.

The present-day classification system began as an Army system in World War I and finally was codified by an executive order issued in 1940 by President Roosevelt. The noxious weed of secrecy in the name of national security really began its fast-spreading growth with President Truman's Executive Order 10290, and it was fertilized to full bloom by President Eisenhower's Executive Order 10501 in 1955.

None of these executive directives on information important to the nation's security was based on any specific statutory grant of power. They referred only to the President's power as commander-in-chief under the Constitution and to the "statutes" in general.

The Freedom of Information Law granted statutory authority for government secrecy in the name of national security. It stated, for the first time in any statute, that public records could be withheld if they contained information "specifically required

RESULTS OF ADMINISTRATIVE APPEALS AND COURT ACTION UNDER 5 USC 552*
Period Covering July 4, 1967 to July 4, 1971

Access to public records refused, in whole or in part	2,195 instances
Refusal administratively appealed	296 instances
Refusal sustained on appeal	196 instances
Refusal reversed on appeal, in whole or in part	79 instances
Appeal pending	21 instances
Court action initiated	99 instances
Refusal sustained in court	24 instances
Refusal reversed in court, in whole or in part	32 instances
Court action pending	44 instances

* Source: Hearings, March, 1972, Foreign Operations and Government Information Subcommittee — Administration and Operation of the Freedom of Information Act, pp. 1338-1339.

by executive order to be kept secret in the interest of national defense or foreign policy." The Department of Justice seriously considered proposing a new executive order — replacing 10501 issued by President Eisenhower and continued in force by Presidents Kennedy and Johnson — when the Freedom of Information Law was enacted. Instead, they created a committee and studied the problem.

As the administration changed hands, the committee evolved into a legal-military group supervised by David Young in the White House, one of the Presidential assistants who apparently had many other interesting duties and left his place of employment in the wake of the Watergate scandal. The committee proposed many major revisions in the system for classifying and protecting national defense information, and the new system was incorporated by President Nixon into Executive Order 11652.

President Nixon, like his predecessors, relied on the Constitution in the preamble to his executive order, and, for the first time, he referred to a specific congressional grant of authority — the Freedom of Information Law. President Nixon's Executive Order 11652 took a step toward recognizing congressional authority to set up, by statute, a system to classify and protect national security information, and it made many other changes in the classification system.

For the first time since classification of national security information was regularized in 1940, the presidential directive set up an appeal procedure which might give the press and the public a tool to dig out documents that the military and foreign service officers would rather keep hidden.

The Nixon Order also wound down the secrecy time clock, reducing to ten years the period during which many top secret documents will be hidden and reducing the secret and confidential periods to eight years and six years. But the order also sets up a system to by-pass automatic declassification if a top official specifies in writing the reason for an exception to the rules.

The new executive order drastically reduced the number of government agencies given authority to use secrecy stamps and required each official with stamping power to be so designated by his boss, in writing. The watchdog committee, appointed by Nixon to oversee the new executive order, reported a 63 percent reduction in the number of bureaucrats wielding secrecy stamps within two months after the new order took effect. The committee said, however, more than 16,000 government employees still have the power to put classification stamps on documents.

The committee also will handle appeals from the public about overclassification or too slow declassification and has the power to enforce Nixon's promise that the burden of proof that secrecy is necessary will be put on the classifiers. Whether the new rules against misuse of secrecy stamps will be enforced any better than the old rules is questionable in view of a recent study of four years of enforcement of secrecy regulations.

The study reports that there were 2,433 investigations by government security experts of violations of regulations governing the handling of national security information and that administrative penalties — ranging from reprimands to loss of pay — were assessed against 2,504 individuals. However, only two of the investigations involved *overclassification* where too high a security stamp was stuck on a government document and none — not a single one — of the administrative penalties was assessed for violating the presidential directive that "overclassification shall be scrupulously avoided."

"Now the White House reports that the number of persons authorized to stamp documents has been reduced," Congressman William Moorhead commented. "That is a step forward, but only a small step when the fact is that earlier directives prohibiting overclassification never were enforced. Reducing the number of persons who can wield the classification stamps is fine, but increasing the penalties for overclassification is useless — two times zero still is zero."

There are two major problems with the present system for classifying national security information: there is no penalty for overclassification, and the system has no statutory base. While President Nixon did bow toward the Freedom of Information Law, he did not seek statutory authority for the classification system.

Instead, the Nixon Administration asked Congress to revise the espionage laws to make it a felony to disclose any information, whether or not the information was properly "classified." The Administration's bill S.1400 — would give all agency regulations issued under past, present or future executive orders the force of law. Thus, a rubber stamp on a government record would replace the present espionage laws as criteria for determining whether past or present public servants disclosed information which damaged the national security.

Worse, the Nixon Administration proposal would delete the present requirements that the government must prove that a person accused under the espionage laws intended, or had reason to believe, that his actions would injure the nation. And the Administration's proposal would prohibit the communication of "classified" information "to a person or the general public" — an obvious attempt to plug leaks to members of Congress and the press.

Instead of proposing legislation to stretch the espionage laws over all government information and over all possible recipients, whether or not there was intent to injure the United States, the Nixon Administration should ask Congress to look carefully at the present system for classifying information in the name of national security. Hopefully, Congress would establish a classification system by law, instead of by executive fiat, and the law would include penalties for all abuses of the system — overclassification as well as underclassification.

V

There is one facet of the government information problem where no President can be expected to propose legislative action — the claim of "executive privilege." Presidents since George Washington have claimed a right, under the separation of powers doctrine and the "take care" clause of the Constitution, to control access to their personal records of office and to have the power to withhold information from the press and the public — usually, the President's commander-in-chief authority is cited — and there has been reliance on a constitutional power to withhold information from the courts, usually citing the separation of powers doctrine. But the claim of "executive privilege," which has caused the major controversies in recent years, is a claim of constitutional power to withhold information from the Congress when it is functioning as a basic part of the governmental process and is most in need of information.

"Executive privilege," exercised against the Congress, became a popular political issue in the Eisenhower Administration. During the Army-McCarthy Hearings, President Eisenhower directed his Secretary of Defense and the Secretary's subordinates to refuse to testify about advisory communications during the hearings. This claim of an "executive privilege," exercised in a single instance in connection with a single hearing, became a broad shield of secrecy which officials in the Eisenhower Administration raised against cooperation with the Congress in at least 34 separate instances.

President Kennedy faced the problem early in his administration and followed the procedure of President Eisenhower with one important difference. When a Senate subcommittee held hearings on the

Defense Department's system for editing speeches of military leaders, President Kennedy directed witnesses to refuse to identify the military editors who had blue-penciled specific speeches. But he said that his directive could not become blanket authority to use the claim of "executive privilege" throughout the Executive Branch as had been done in the Eisenhower years. "Executive privilege," he said, could be used only by the President and would not be invoked without presidential approval.

President Johnson and President Nixon announced they would follow the Kennedy precedent and limit the exercise of "executive privilege" against Congress to a personal, presidential privilege. President Nixon even issued a memorandum setting up a procedure for routing refusals of congressional information through the Department of Justice and to the President's White House counsel.

But the limitation did not work. President Kennedy exercised a personal "executive privilege" once, in connection with the military censorship hearings, but officials in his administration refused to provide information requested by congressional committee three additional times. President Johnson did not personally exercise "executive privilege," but Johnson Administration officials twice refused documents or testimony to congressional committees. President Nixon used "executive privilege" to personally refuse information to Congress in four instances, but officials in his administration refused documents or testimony to congressional committees in 15 additional instances.

These 20 instances of Executive Branch refusal of information to Congress in the face of a presidential statement that "executive privilege" is a personal prerogative were not refusals based on some staff, advisory relationship with the President.

There was no lawyer-client relationship involved. Each of the 20 refusals of information to Congress came from an official, appointed with the advice and consent of the Senate or an official of an agency or department created by the Congress.

Is it possible that, in 20 instances, three presidents had issued secret directives to refuse information to Congress? Is it possible that, in 20 instances, Executive Branch officials had decided to violate their commander-in-chief's directive that the invocation of "executive privilege" was a presidential power? No, it is much more likely that, in 20 instances, Executive Branch officials were taking advantage of the fact that Congress is a diverse and uncoordinated branch of government which has not established clear procedures to require cooperation from the Executive Branch.

Each of the 20 instances was a publicly-reported case of a House or Senate committee requesting Executive Branch documents or testimony, but in none of the 20 instances was there a clear confrontation between the two branches of the Federal Government. There may have been a subpoena issued in a very few cases or there may have been a committee vote to require testimony or documents, but the subpoena was not pushed and the committee vote was not forcefully and publicly transmitted to the President.

There is no law which requires Executive Branch officials to respond to requests for information from the Congress. Without such a law, those officials who do not wish to cooperate can force congressional committees to make a major issue of refusals of information. That, apparently, is what happened in the 20 instances, and in each instance the congressional committee decided that the issue was not worth the effort.

A law requiring agencies and officials of the Executive Branch outside the White House to furnish information to any committee of Congress certainly would not prevent all abuse of the claim of "executive privilege." It would not settle the question of testimony by the President's personal advisers; it would not prevent the President from wrapping his personal claim of "executive privilege" around any government employee. These are issues which the courts have refused to settle and, possibly, should not settle to maintain the delicate balance between the three coordinate branches of the Federal Government.

If, however, the controversy over official access to important government information can be limited to a conflict between the President, the Congress and the courts, a major part of the problem will be solved. If the Legislative Branch should require, by law, that the huge bureaucracy — a creature created by the Congress — can be required, by law, to provide information to Congress, unless the President personally asserts this claim of "executive privilege," the lines of battle will be clearly drawn.

And Congress would win the most important battle: the fight to get the facts of government it needs to set the legislative policies, without using its ultimate weapon of cutting off funds and abolishing the programs established to carry out its policies.

VI

The other side of the government information problem — the positive flow of information through the government's public relations machinery — is at least as complicated as the various aspects of negative restrictions on press and public access to the facts of government. Part of the complication is that "public relations" are two dirty words in the Federal Government. President Richard M. Nixon helped make it so in 1970 when he ordered agencies to curtail "self-serving and wasteful public relations activities." After a minor bureaucratic flurry producing a report that the government had 6,144 full-time public relations employees, the Nixon drive against self-serving government publicity died out. President Nixon certainly was not the first politician to use government information experts as whipping boys. In fact, a 1913 federal statute prohibiting the employment of "publicity experts" unless Congress specifically appropriates funds for the jobs, still is the law of the land.

That law came about because a government agency told the truth. The Civil Service Commission put out a help-wanted ad for the new office of public roads. They asked for a publicity expert whose contact with newspaper writers and publishers was broad enough "to insure publication of the items prepared by him." Congressman Gillett of Massachusetts was offended by the forthright approach of the ad and pushed through a rider on an appropriation act which has become the federal statute prohibiting the hiring of publicity experts.

Thus, none of the 6,000 plus full-time public relations persons in the federal government is called a public relations person, nor a publicity agent, nor a press agent, nor a publicist, nor anything truly descriptive of their real jobs. They are public information specialists, or editorial assistants, or public affairs officers.

These employees are only part of the thousands of federal officials who spend much of their time making speeches, attending meetings, writing articles and handling the other work necessary to explain a government program to the public. The 6,000 are the full-time professionals, and the huge majority of them are under the civil service system, supposedly protected from partisan political pressures.

At the very tip of the government information iceberg are the individuals who head the public relations operations of the executive departments and independent agencies. These top-level government publicists were pinpointed by the directors of the government agencies in answer to a 1971 letter from Congressman William Moorhead to the head of each executive department and independent agency asking for a current biography of each "director, deputy director, assistant or other top level information officer in every bureau, division, branch or other constituent unit" of the agency.

Who are these top level information employees? What are their qualifications? How did they get where they are? The biographies provided by the government agencies covered some 400 public information bureau heads and their deputies, and offer a composite picture of the expert who runs the day-to-day government information programs. He is:

- a man who has a college degree and has probably done some graduate work;
- a man who has spent much of his professional life as a reporter for a newspaper or broadcasting station;
- a man who owes his government information job to the Nixon Administration.

By far the greatest number of top-level government information experts are male. In fact, sexism rears its ugly head much higher in federal government information offices than in federal offices where the employees handle other white collar professional jobs.

Almost one-third of the full time, white collar federal employees — GS 13 and above — are female. More than six percent of all federal lawyers are female. But only three percent of the top federal public information professionals are female, and very few of them are bureau heads.

Male college graduates are not as scarce as women in federal information offices. Nearly half of the top information officers held a college degree and another 40 percent had an advanced degree or have done work toward one.

More government information experts have moved into their current profession through journalism — news reporting or editing — than by any other route. This is not surprising since the top level government publicist must direct his agency's daily dealing with reporters. But the number of publicity promoters whose primary background is public relations or advertising is growing under the Nixon Administration. Only eight percent of the federal information experts who were on the job before President Nixon's inauguration in January, 1969 had a primary background in public relations. Of those information experts who were appointed or promoted by the Nixon Administration, 19 percent are public relations professionals.

The Washington image machine is run by public information people who were appointed or promoted by the Nixon Administration. Fifty-one percent of the top level federal information employees were in that category in 1971. Even if the Nixon appointees in the Executive Office of the President are excluded, the proportion of information experts, who were appointed or promoted during the first two and one-half years of the Nixon Administration, still is 50 percent and the proportion has grown as the administration has continued in office.

There is no evidence that Herb Klein, as the government's Director of Communications, has been placing political appointees in civil service informational jobs. His function in the early Nixon years was to coordinate the activities of the top-level press agents for cabinet members and to get the Nixon Administration story out to the editors and publishers of the news media outside of Washington. Ronald Ziegler, as press secretary, handled the White House press corps, and others in the White House were responsible for getting jobs at the civil service level for the faithful.

Later, Herb Klein became the number one surrogate for President Nixon, making speeches and holding press conferences around the country. As Herb Klein moved out, his deputy, Ken Clawson, moved into the information-directing job, telling the civil service information professionals how to write speeches and how to put out other propaganda extolling the virtues of Nixon's budget-cutting programs and attacking Congress for trying to spend money.

While Herb Klein's operation was the first time that a coordinated program of government-wide publicity ever was acknowledged, there have been attempts in past administrations to make the public information operations in government agencies a part of the political publicity machine directed from the White House. There were two attempts in the Kennedy Administration to convince the civil service public information experts in the government agencies that they should refer regularly to the President when they put out press releases about their agency programs. A Peace Corps publicist was transferred to the White House in 1962 and given the job of "coordinating" government agency publicity from the White House. He was unsuccessful and went on to his reward as head of publicity for another new government agency. Another former newsman was transferred into the White House information coordination job but he, too, found the problem too big to solve.

Neither of these Kennedy Administration appointees ever surfaced. Not until Herbert Klein was appointed as the government's first Director of Communications did the White House ever admit that someone was looking over the shoulders of the civil servants hired to inform the public about government agency activities. Not until Deputy Director of Communications Ken Clawson set up a government-wide political propaganda drive did Congress begin to look carefully at the potential danger of an official Ministry of Truth.

In April, 1973, legislation was introduced to help solve the problem of availability of information from the Federal Government. This bill—H.R. 7268 by Congressman Moorhead — is in addition to the legislation already under way to improve the Freedom of Information Law, and it is an extremely unusual proposal. Instead of prohibiting a government-wide coordination of public information activities, instead of using the negative approach of the 1913 law restricting publicity experts or the 1970 Nixon order against self-serving public relations, the bill recognizes that public information experts in top-level government positions can serve an important function in a democratic society.

The bill would create a chief public information officer at the level of Assistant Secretary in every department and agency of the Federal Government. At present, information activities are administered at the Assistant Secretary level only in the Defense, State, and Health, Education and Welfare Departments and the National Aeronautics and Space Administration. In all other government activities outside the White House, the man who is responsible for public knowledge of the public's business is too far down the administrative line to carry any weight in the councils of government. He handles routine press releases, while a political appointee hidden under a euphemistic title tries to do the real public relations for the agency.

The bill would direct the chief public information officer to handle all requests and make all decisions — subject to the approval of the head of the agency — under the Freedom of Information Law. At present, this work is done in the public information offices of only a handful of government agencies. In all the rest, decisions on public access to government information are made by program administrators or lawyers whose professional expertise is valuable, but whose view of the public's need to know is narrow.

However, this novel approach to government public relations — openly recognizing that every government agency has a responsibility to inform the public and establishing a top-level office to do the job — carries with it the concomitant danger of setting up a government-wide propaganda machine controlled from the White House. The proposed chief public information officer certainly would be a political appointee and would be as interested in the welfare of the administration temporarily in power as in the dissemination of factual information about his agency.

But there already is coordination of government information from the White House — there was long before the 1913 law; there always will be. It is hidden under phony titles and fuzzy lines of authority. To bring it out into the open would permit Congress, the press and the public to hold public relations professionals responsible for the government's public information. In a democratic society, the people's right to know cannot be left to amateurs.

Minor improvements in the Freedom of Information Law and a major overhaul of government information programs might bring our system closer to the ideal proposed by the leading philosopher of public information, who was one of the creators of our form of government.

At every convention of journalists, someone always quotes Thomas Jefferson, but they usually quote only part of his comment on the role of the press in a democratic society:

> The basis of our government's being the opinion of the people, the very first object should be to keep that right; and were it left for me to decide whether we should have a government without newspapers, or newspapers without a government, I should not hesitate for a moment to prefer the latter. *But I should mean that every man should receive those papers and be capable of reading them.* (Italics added.)

In this modern age of mass communication, Thomas Jefferson's caveat to his newspapers-without-government comment no doubt would call for the strongest possible information laws as tools for the Congress, the public and the press, to enable them to dig out the facts of government and to help them do their jobs in a well-informed democratic society.

To recapitulate, the actions advocated to help achieve those ends are:

● Amend the Freedom of Information Law to require the federal bureaucracy to act expeditiously and honestly on requests for public record; to narrow the few existing loopholes in the law; and to force the agencies to respond immediately to public demands for government information;

● Require government payment of legitimate legal fees incurred in taking a freedom of information case to court, thus making it possible for more citizens to force more agencies to prove the need for secrecy;

● Permit the courts to exercise an independent judgment on whether information, classified as important to the national security, truly is important;

● Set up a system for classifying and protecting national security information by statute, providing penalties for overclassification as well as underclassification, but retaining the present provision that violation of the espionage laws can be based only upon intent to damage the United States of America;

● Establish a chief public information officer in every agency of the Federal Government, responsible to Congress and the public, as well as to his political superior;

● Adopt a law requiring every Executive Branch official outside the White House to provide information requested by Congress, thus effectively limiting the claim of "executive privilege" to a personal, presidential assertion.

ANNUAL CHIEF JUSTICE EARL WARREN CONFERENCE ON ADVOCACY IN THE UNITED STATES / 1973

HERBERT H. BENNETT
President
Roscoe Pound-American Trial Lawyers Foundation

THEODORE I. KOSKOFF
Chairman
Annual Chief Justice Earl Warren Conference
on Advocacy

STANLEY E. PREISER and JACK A. TRAVIS, JR.
Co-Chairmen
Annual Chief Justice Earl Warren Conference
on Advocacy

Conference Advisor
PROFESSOR THOMAS I. EMERSON
Lines Professor of Law, Yale Law School

Background Papers:
PROFESSOR BENNO C. SCHMIDT, JR.
Professor of Law, Columbia University
School of Law

Subject: JOURNALISTS' PRIVILEGE: ONE
YEAR AFTER BRANZBURG

PROFESSOR SIG MICKELSON
Professor of Journalism, The Medill School of
Journalism, Northwestern University

Subject: THE FIRST AMENDMENT AND
BROADCAST JOURNALISM

PROFESSOR SAMUEL J. ARCHIBALD
Professor, Department of Communication,
American University

Subject: ACCESS TO GOVERNMENT
INFORMATION — THE RIGHT BEFORE
THE FIRST AMENDMENT

Group Chairmen

PROFESSOR DAVID HABER

Professor of Law, Rutgers University School of Law, The State University of New Jersey; since 1946 has taught law; co-author of several books; Law Clerk to Mr. Justice Hugo L. Black, Supreme Court of the United States

PROFESSOR BARBARA D. UNDERWOOD

Assistant Professor, Yale Law School; Law Clerk to Mr. Justice Thurgood Marshall, Supreme Court of the United States, 1971-72; Law Clerk to Chief Judge David L. Bazelon, U.S. Court of Appeals, D.C. Circuit, 1969-71

THE HONORABLE GEORGE W. WOOD

Judge, Intermediate Court, Kanawha County, Charleston, West Virginia

Group Reporters

PROFESSOR ELIOT A. LANDAU

Assisstant Professor, Drake University Law School; Chairman, Section on Law and Journalism, Association of American Law Schools; Co-chairman, Council on Law and Journalism

PROFESSOR ROBERT M. O'NEIL

Professor of Law, Vice President and Provost for Academic Affairs, University of Cincinnati; active in area of educational opportunities; author of numerous articles and several books; Law Clerk to Mr. Justice William J. Brennan, Jr., Supreme Court of the United States

RONALD L. PLESSER

Director, Press Information Center (established jointly by National Press Club and Ralph Nader); attorney associated with Ralph Nader's Center for the Study of Responsive Law

Conferees

DEAN ELIE ABEL
New York, New York

Dean, Columbia University Graduate School of Journalism; past reporter-commentator, NBC News; former Washington and foreign correspondent, *The New York Times*

DEAN JEROME A. BARRON
Syracuse, New York

Dean, College of Law, Syracuse University; co-author of "Mass Communication Law" and many articles on communication law; author of recent book, "Freedom of Press for Whom?"

LAWRENCE M. BASKIR
Washington, D.C.

Chief Counsel and Staff Director, Constitutional Rights Subcommittee, U.S. Senate; Adjunct Professor, Georgetown University Law Center and Columbus Law School of Catholic University

PROFESSOR VINCENT A. BLASI
Ann Arbor, Michigan

Professor, University of Michigan Law School; specialist on the First Amendment; author of "Press Subpoenas: An Empirical and Legal Analysis," *Michigan Law Review*; draftsman of the proposed Uniform Reporter's Privilege Act

PAUL M. BRANZBURG
Detroit, Michigan
> Investigative Reporter, *Detroit Free Press*; attorney; petitioner in U.S. Supreme Court decision, *Branzburg v. Hayes,* in conjunction with his investigative reporting for *Louisville Courier-Journal*

ROBERT CLARKE BROWN
Cambridge, Massachusetts
> Law Student, Harvard Law School; Managing Editor, *Harvard Civil Rights-Civil Liberties Law Review*

WILLIAM J. CALDWELL
Portland, Maine
> Editorial Page Editor, *Maine Sunday Telegram;* former Director of Information for Foreign Operations during both Eisenhower Administrations

BERT CASE
Jackson, Mississippi
> News Director, WAPT-TV, Jackson, Mississippi (ABC-TV affiliate)

PROFESSOR MARSHALL COHEN
New York, New York
> Professor of Philosophy, City University of New York; Editor of *Philosophy and Public Affairs;* member of the (Goodell) Committee for the Study of Incarceration; publishes widely in legal, literary and philosophical journals

ELIZABETH RYAN COLE
West Newton, Massachusetts
> Law Student, Boston University School of Law; worked with Law Students Civil Rights Research Committee (Flym, Geller, Miller, Taylor Law Commune)

EDWARD R. CONY
New York, New York
> Vice President and Executive Editor, *The Wall Street Journal;* recipient of Pulitzer Prize for National Affairs Reporting; reporter and editor for *The Wall Street Journal* for twenty years

THOMAS I. EMERSON
New Haven, Connecticut
> Lines Professor of Law, Yale Law School; among his scholarly writings are "The System of Freedom of Expression" and "Toward a General Theory of the First Amendment"

DEAN ROY M. FISHER
Columbia, Missouri
> Dean, University of Missouri School of Journalism; twenty years with *The Chicago Daily News;* five years as editor, during which time the newspaper was awarded two Pulitzer Prizes

REV. DR. WILLIAM F. FORE
New York, New York
> Executive Director, Broadcasting and Film Commission, National Council of Churches and Assistant General Secretary, National Council of Churches

JOHN FRASCA
Tampa, Florida
> Investigative reporter; author; Pulitzer Prize winner for investigative reporting; recipient of numerous awards including the Edgar Allen Poe Award

ALFRED FRIENDLY, JR.
Washington, D.C.
> Counsel to the Intergovernmental Relations Subcommittee, U.S. Senate Government Operations Committee; former correspondent for *The New York Times* and *Newsweek Magazine*

PROFESSOR DAVID HABER
Newark, New Jersey
> Professor of Law, Rutgers University School of Law, The State University of New Jersey; since 1946 has taught law; co-author of several books; Law Clerk to Mr. Justice Hugo L. Black, Supreme Court of the United States

ARTHUR B. HANSON
Washington, D.C.
> General Counsel, American Newspaper Publishers Association; appointed to Reserve Forces Policy Board, U.S. Department of Defense for 1971-1974 by former Secretary of Defense, Melvin Laird

I. WILLIAM HILL
Washington, D.C.
> Associate Editor, *The Washington Star-News;* former President, Associated Press Managing Editors Assn.; one of American Society of Newspaper Editors to visit the People's Republic of China in October 1972

PROFESSOR SAMUEL B. HOROVITZ
Boston, Massachusetts
> Professor, Suffolk University Law School; former Commissioner, National Commission on State Workmen's Compensation Laws

PROFESSOR SAMUEL KRISLOV
Minneapolis, Minnesota
> Professor, Dept. of Political Science, University of Minnesota; Ford Foundation Faculty Fellowship, 1972-73; researcher, professor and lecturer in law, social science and political science

L. JAMES KRONFELD
Washington, D.C.
> Counsel, Foreign Operations and Government Information Subcommittee, U.S. House Government Operations Committee; formerly Legislative Counsel and Executive Assistant for U.S. Representatives in Washington, D.C.

PROFESSOR ELIOT A. LANDAU
Des Moines, Iowa
> Assistant Professor, Drake University Law School; Chairman, Section on Law and Journalism, Association of American Law Schools; Co-chairman, Council on Law and Journalism

JACK C. LANDAU
Washington, D.C.
> Reporter covering the Supreme Court of the United States, Newhouse Newspapers; Steering Committee, The Reporters Committee for Freedom of the Press

ROBERT F. LEONARD
Flint, Michigan
> Prosecuting Attorney, Genesee County; Treasurer, National District Attorneys Assn.; originator of a variety of citizen action programs, subsequently adopted by other states

DAVID LIGHTMAN
Baltimore, Maryland
> Reporter, *The Evening Sun;* held in contempt for refusing to disclose to Worcester County grand jury source of information regarding the sale of drugs

JOHN T. McCUTCHEON, JR.
Chicago, Illinois
> Editor, Editorial Page, *Chicago Tribune;* twenty-eight year career with the *Chicago Tribune;* editorial writer for past sixteen years

PETER S. McGHEE
Boston, Massachusetts
Executive Editor, "The Advocates," WGBH-TV (New England Educational TV Outlet); recipient of Emmy Award 1973 for "The Advocates" program on newsmen's privilege; formerly producer of documentaries at National Educational Television in New York

JAMES C. MILLSTONE
St. Louis, Missouri
Assistant Managing Editor, *St. Louis Post-Dispatch;* Washington Correspondent for *Post-Dispatch* for seven years covering the Supreme Court of the United States and civil rights movement

PROFESSOR HENRY P. MONAGHAN
Boston, Massachusetts
Professor, Boston University School of Law; since 1963 has taught law

WILLIAM G. MULLEN
Washington, D.C.
General Counsel and Secretary, National Newspaper Assn.; former Corporation Counsel for the City of Joliet, Illinois; previously Director of Professional Services, Illinois State Bar Association

PROFESSOR NATHANIEL L. NATHANSON
Chicago, Illinois
Vose Professor of Law, Northwestern University; professor and lecturer in the U.S. and abroad; former member, Administrative Conference of the United States; Law Clerk to Mr. Justice Louis B. Brandeis, Supreme Court of the United States

ARTHUR NORTH
Boston, Massachusetts
Editorial and Political Affairs Director, WNAC-TV, Boston, Mass. (CBS-TV affiliate); former reporter, editor and editorial writer, *N.Y. News;* Asst. Manager, Newspaper Information Service, American Newspaper Publishers Association

PROFESSOR ROBERT M. O'NEIL
Cincinnati, Ohio
Professor of Law, Vice President and Provost for Academic Affairs, University of Cincinnati; active in area of educational opportunities; author of numerous articles and several books; Law Clerk to Mr. Justice William J. Brennan, Supreme Court of the United States

PAUL PAPPAS
Providence, Rhode Island
Reporter-photographer, WTEV-TV, New Bedford, Mass. (ABC-TV affiliate); subpoenaed by a grand jury to disclose information regarding the Black Panthers; Caldwell-Branzburg-Pappas case carried to the Supreme Court of the United States

LAWRENCE PICKARD
Boston, Massachusetts
Director of News and Public Affairs, WCVB-TV (ABC-TV affiliate); News Editor, ABC-TV Evening News, and Anchor Editor with Special Events Unit handling space shots and elections; Managing Editor, NBC "Today" Show; Producer, CBS Newsfilm

RONALD L. PLESSER
Washington, D.C.
Director, Press Information Center (established jointly by National Press Club and Ralph Nader); attorney associated with Ralph Nader's Center for the Study of Responsive Law

THE HONORABLE CHARLES A. POMEROY
Portland, Maine
Associate Justice of the Maine Supreme Judicial Court

L. A. (SCOT) POWE, JR.
Austin, Texas
Assistant Professor, School of Law, The University of Texas at Austin; Law Clerk to Mr. Justice William O. Douglas, Supreme Court of the United States

DONALD K. POWERS
Portland, Maine
> Station Manager, WCSH-TV, Portland, Me. (NBC-TV affiliate); varied experience in creative and administrative work of broadcast stations

E. BARRETT PRETTYMAN, JR.
Washington, D.C.
> Attorney for Paul Pappas before the Supreme Court of the United States (Caldwell-Branzburg-Pappas cases); Law Clerk to Hon. Robert A. Jackson, Hon. Felix Frankfurter and Hon. John M. Harlan, Justices of the Supreme Court of the United States; author; former reporter

JOHN C. QUINN
Rochester, New York
> Vice President/News of Gannett Company, Inc., working with Gannett Group editors and publishers to develop news talent and resources for newspaper chain; President, Associated Press Managing Editors Association

PROFESSOR ALBERT J. ROSENTHAL
New York, New York
> Professor, Columbia University School of Law; author of numerous articles; Law Clerk to Mr. Justice Felix Frankfurter, Supreme Court of the United States

CHARLES R. SANFORD
Portland, Maine
> Vice President and General Manager, WGAN Radio (AM and FM) and WGAN-TV, Portland, Me. (CBS-TV affiliate); member of Board of Directors, Guy Gannett Broadcasting Services

WILLIAM C. SEXTON
Long Island, New York
> Associate Editor of *Newsday* in charge of Editorial and Op-Ed pages; UPI staff for 15 years in editing, reporting and administrative posts, including bureau manager in London and New York; former Asso. Director, American Press Institute

PROFESSOR MARTIN SHAPIRO
Cambridge, Massachusetts
> Professor, Dept. of Government, Harvard University; author of several books on the Supreme Court of the United States, constitutional law and American government and politics, including "Freedom of Speech: The Supreme Court and Judicial Review"

JOHN H. F. SHATTUCK
New York, New York
> National Staff Counsel, American Civil Liberties Union; ACLU witness before congressional subcommittees in hearings on privacy, data collection and government secrecy litigation; author of articles on constitutional law and civil liberties

H. L. STEVENSON
New York, New York
> Editor-in-Chief and Vice President, United Press International; former UPI Southern Division News Manager in Atlanta, covering major civil rights stories in the South from 1953 to 1963

STUART F. SUCHERMAN
New York, New York
> Program Officer, Office of Public Broadcasting, The Ford Foundation, developing alternative communication policies in the U.S.; lecturer and author on cable television; formerly Assistant General Counsel, National Educational Television

JOHN C. SUMBERG
New Haven, Connecticut
> Law student, Yale Law School; Editor, *The Yale Review of Law and Social Action*; author of "Note on the Right of Non-English Speaking Persons to Receive Legal Notices in their own Language" for *Yale Law Journal*; New Haven Legal Aid

WM. DAVIS TAYLOR
Boston, Massachusetts
    Publisher and Chairman of the Board, Globe
    Newspaper Company; Chairman and Director,
    American Newspaper Publishers Assn.; recipi-
    ent, Honorary Doctor of Law, Colby College

PROFESSOR BARBARA D. UNDERWOOD
New Haven, Connecticut
    Assistant Professor, Yale Law School; Law
    Clerk to Mr. Justice Thurgood Marshall, Su-
    preme Court of the United States, 1971-72;
    Law Clerk to Chief Judge David L. Bazelon,
    U.S. Court of Appeals, D.C. Circuit, 1969-71

NICHOLAS von HOFFMAN
Washington, D.C.
    National columnist, *The Washington Post* and
    King Features Syndicate; former staff member,
    Chicago Daily News; author of book, "We Are
    the People Our Parents Warned Us Against,"
    among others

WARREN WEAVER, JR.
Washington, D.C.
    Reporter, Washington Bureau of *The New York
    Times,* covering the Supreme Court of the
    United States, federal judicial system and legal
    profession; lawyer; among books authored —
    "Both Your Houses"; preparing book on role
    of media in political campaigning

TRACY A. WESTEN
Washington, D.C.
    Director, Stern Community Law Firm; former-
    ly legal assistant to Comm. Nicholas Johnson,
    Federal Communications Commission; among
    publications — Johnson & Westen, "A Twen-
    tieth-Century Soapbox: The Right to Purchase
    Radio and Television Time"

CHARLES L. WHIPPLE
Boston, Massachusetts
    Editor, Editorial Page, *The Boston Globe;* as
    reporter specialized in political corruption and
    court cases; recipient of UPI first prize award
    for editorial "Our Free Press in Danger," 1971;
    wrote series of editorials published as "The
    People's Need to Know," 1973

THOMAS H. WOLF
New York, New York
    Vice President and Director of Television Public
    Affairs, ABC News; ABC News specials under
    his supervision received nearly 40 awards for
    excellence, including five George Foster Pea-
    body awards; veteran newspaperman

THE HONORABLE GEORGE W. WOOD
Charleston, West Virginia
    Judge, Intermediate Court, Kanawha County,
    Charleston, West Virginia

Establishment of the
Annual Chief Justice Earl Warren Conference
on Advocacy in the United States

On September 28, 1968, Earl Warren, Chief Justice of the United States, laid the cornerstone of the Roscoe Pound-American Trial Lawyers Law and Research Center in Cambridge, Massachusetts.

At that time the Foundation announced its intention to create an Annual Chief Justice Earl Warren Conference on Advocacy. The text of the resolution formulating the Conference follows:

BE IT RESOLVED that the Foundation do and hereby does establish a fund, the income of which shall be sufficient to conduct an Annual Conference on trial law and practice and the role of the trial lawyer in America.

Its invited participants shall be leaders in thought or action in the law who are concerned with the quality, purposes and societal contributions of advocacy in America, along with such members of such other related professions and pursuits as shall be deemed appropriate.

The Annual Conference shall be known as the Chief Justice Earl Warren Annual Conference on Advocacy in the United States.

The general purpose of each Conference shall be the assessment of the trends, the accomplishments and failures, if any, of advocacy to meet society's on-going demands upon it as of the time of each Annual Conference, and to chart ways in which the trial lawyer, in each forthcoming year, can, either through short-range or long-range action, align the practice of trial law with the needs of modern society, taking into account newly-developing social instruments and programs, in order to ensure the thorough protection of the law for all American citizens.

The studies and findings of each Conference shall be published and widely disseminated and appropriate action then taken to encourage the implementation of its recommendations.

LIFETIME FELLOWS OF THE FOUNDATION

The Lifetime Fellows of the Roscoe Pound-American Trial Lawyers Foundation are recognized for their continuous support of research endeavors in the intensive pursuit of truth for the ultimate goal of more effective administration of justice for all.

James S. Abatiell
Rutland, Vermont

James H. Ackerman
Long Beach, California

Thomas T. Anderson
Indio, California

Ashcraft & Gerel
Washington, D.C.

William I. Aynes
Atlanta, Georgia

Russell M. Baker
Dallas, Texas

Joseph G. Barbieri
Elizabeth, New Jersey

A. William Barlow
Honolulu, Hawaii

Herbert H. Bennett
Portland, Maine

Ralph R. Benson
Hollywood, California

Charles F. Blanchard
Raleigh, North Carolina

Milton M. Blumenthal
Chicago, Illinois

George A. Boyle
Bakersfield, California

Ellis B. Brannon
Cleveland, Ohio

Louis T. Brindisi
Utica, New York

Walter W. Brooks
Columbia, South Carolina

Evan H. Callanan
Westland, Michigan

Richard J. Cardali
New York, New York

Jessie B. Carnevale
Tucson, Arizona

Rex Carr
East St. Louis, Illinois

Clinton W. Chapman
Washington, D.C.

Samuel Charfoos
Southfield, Michigan

Edward H. Cloutier
Livermore Falls, Maine

Arthur Cobb
Baton Rouge, Louisiana

LIFETIME FELLOWS OF THE FOUNDATION

Al J. Cone
West Palm Beach, Florida

Bobby Lee Cook
Summerville, Georgia

James E. Coonley, II
Hampton, Iowa

John F. Corcoran
Tucson, Arizona

Roy Daubenspeck
Plaistow, New Hampshire

Peter A. Davis
Ann Arbor, Michigan

Robert R. Disbro
Cleveland, Ohio

John E. Dolan, Jr.
Patchogue, New York

Joseph C. Dwyer
Olean, New York

J. Robert Dyment
San Diego, California

Irving M. Einbinder
Hagerstown, Maryland

Arnold B. Elkind
New York, New York

J. Newton Esdaile
Boston, Massachusetts

Donald J. Farage
Philadelphia, Pennsylvania

Moody M. Farhart
Minot, North Dakota

Millard C. Farmer, Jr.
Newnan, Georgia

Albert S. Fein
Philadelphia, Pennsylvania

Philip R. Finkelmeier
Cincinnati, Ohio

Richard S. Fleisher
Chicago, Illinois

Abraham E. Freedman
Philadelphia, Pennsylvania

Philip S. Frey
Honolulu, Hawaii

Lawrence B. Friedman
North Miami Beach, Florida

Jacob D. Fuchsberg
New York, New York

E. S. Gallon
Dayton, Ohio

Harold M. Gamer
Beverly Hills, California

John Gardenal
San Francisco, California

John Phillips Godfrey
Many, Louisiana

John Michael Goldberg
Chicago, Illinois

Burl L. Green
Portland, Oregon

Herbert Hafif
Claremont, California

Oliver Wendell Hasenflue
Avon Lake, Ohio

William W. Hawkins
Kingsport, Tennessee

Thomas L. Hennessey
Towson, Maryland

Russ M. Herman
New Orleans, Louisiana

Lawrence P. Hickey
Chicago, Illinois

Arthur C. Hodgson
Lyons, Kansas

Frank D. Holcomb
Marietta, Georgia

John F. Holcomb
Hamilton, Ohio

Herbert B. Hulse
Goldsboro, North Carolina

LIFETIME FELLOWS OF THE FOUNDATION

John K. Hyun
Honolulu, Hawaii

Frank C. Ingraham
Nashville, Tennessee

Hesper A. Jackson, Jr.
Brooklyn, New York

Morris I. Jaffe
Dallas, Texas

Frank Joseph Janik, Jr.
Amherst, Ohio

Joseph L. Jerger
Mansfield, Ohio

William E. Johnson
Frankfort, Kentucky

E. Stewart Jones, Jr.
Troy, New York

Jones, Foster & Loveall
Franklin, Indiana

Leo S. Karlin
Chicago, Illinois

Joseph Kelner
New York, New York

John J. Kennelly
Chicago, Illinois

Sidney B. Klovsky
Philadelphia, Pennsylvania

Elmo E. Koos, Sr.
Peoria, Illinois

Theodore I. Koskoff
Bridgeport, Connecticut

Myron W. Kronisch
Newark, New Jersey

David H. Kubert
Philadelphia, Pennsylvania

Clair William Lane
Tempe, Arizona

Samuel Langerman
Phoenix, Arizona

Max M. Librach
St. Louis, Missouri

George Alexander McKray
San Francisco, California

V. Eugene McMichen
Austell, Georgia

Joseph D. Maher, Jr.
Newark, New Jersey

William Aden Mann
Chevy Chase, Maryland

Richard M. Markus
Cleveland, Ohio

Joe L. Maynes
Aberdeen, South Dakota

Leonard B. Melvin, Jr.
Laurel, Mississippi

Daniel R. Monaco
Naples, Florida

Thomas Owen Morgan
Garden City, New York

Martin J. Murphy
Colorado Springs, Colorado

John E. Norton
Belleville, Illinois

Melvin O. Nuss
Great Bend, Kansas

Cornelius C. O'Brien, Jr.
Philadelphia, Pennsylvania

James P. O'Flarity
Fort Lauderdale, Florida

Dr. Jack H. Olender
Washington, D.C.

Roger L. Pardieck
Seymour, Indiana

Parker, Battaglia, Parker,
Ross and Stolba
St. Petersburg, Florida

Paty, Lawrence & Lawrence
Chattanooga, Tennessee

R. W. Payne, Jr.
Miami, Florida

LIFETIME FELLOWS OF THE FOUNDATION

Rudolph T. Pelletier
Madawaska, Maine

Stephen Andrew Perel
Houston, Texas

Harry M. Pippin
Williston, North Dakota

Paul L. Pratt
East Alton, Illinois

J. Ward Rafferty
New London, Connecticut

Louis J. Richman, Jr.
Newport News, Virginia

Sol Zalel Rosen
Washington, D.C.

Saul I. Ruman
Hammond, Indiana

John W. Russell
Carlinville, Illinois

Stanley E. Sacks
Norfolk, Virginia

E. B. Sahlstrom
Eugene, Oregon

John Burley Scales
Boonville, Indiana

David Schack
New York, New York

George E. Shibley
Long Beach, California

Samuel Shore
Los Angeles, California

Sindell, Sindell, Bourne,
Stern & Spero
Cleveland, Ohio

Abner R. Sisson
Boston, Massachusetts

Cawood Smith
Harlan, Kentucky

Charles W. Smith
Saco, Maine

Craig Spangenberg
Cleveland, Ohio

Robert K. Steinberg
Beverly Hills, California

Stewart & DeChant
Company, L.P.A.
Cleveland, Ohio

Robert C. Strodel
Peoria, Illinois

William Lawrence Summers
Cleveland, Ohio

Glenn J. Tabor
Valparaiso, Indiana

Daniel B. Tallon
Glens Falls, New York

John B. Tittmann
Albuquerque, New Mexico

Jack A. Travis
Jackson, Mississippi

Traxler, Malkoff & Boyd
Company, L.P.A.
Youngstown, Ohio

Edward E. Triviz
Las Cruces, New Mexico

Meyer M. Ucoka
Wailuku, Hawaii

Lewis V. Vafiades
Bangor, Maine

Bill Wagner
Tampa, Florida

Solomon Wasserman
Minneapolis, Minnesota

George F. West, Jr.
Natchez, Mississippi

David E. Williams
Richland, Washington

Williams, Trine and Greenstein
Boulder, Colorado

Robert B. Willson
Asheville, North Carolina

Leon Wolfstone
Seattle, Washington

88